Edgar Cayce (pronounced "Casey"), the greatest mystics America has ever seen is, twenty-two years after his death, a comparative unknown.

There are two reasons for this. The first can be found in the thrust of that serio-comic putdown, "If you're so smart, why aren't you rich?" The average American, horse player or not, finds it impossible to believe that a person such as Edgar Cayce who could look into the future would be unconcerned about making a great deal of money.

The second reason for this mystic's relative obscurity is that some of his most remarkable work was done in medicine, a profession not notoriously hospitable to untrained practitioners. If the doctors who looked to Cayce for help when he lived had given him proportionate credit for their successes, he would not have had to defend himself against the label "charlatan" throughout his working life. Most of the men who were dependent on Cayce when he was alive were afraid to admit even a social association with him.

Because many doctors are now examining Cayce's opinions, many Americans are currently feeling the effect of his existence.

Because of some predictions he made many years ago about what is our immediate future, every American should be aware of him today.

These predictions will have more import after a look at Cayce's past predictions. In considering these past predictions, it is important to keep in mind that they were made while in a self-hypnotic trance-like state by a man whose schooling ended at sixteen, with no training in sociology, geology, history, or government.

. . . In the 1920's Cayce predicted there would be racial strife in the United States just before and after the death of the second of these Presidents.

. . . In 1939 he predicted that two Presidents would

soon die in office. Franklin Roosevelt died in April of 1945 and John Kennedy in November of 1963.

. . . In April of 1929 Cayce predicted a Wall Street crash. It came the following October.

. . . In 1931 he predicted that there would soon be an upturn in the country's fortunes and that "in the spring of '33 will be the real definite improvements." Those "real definite improvements" followed the inauguration of Franklin Roosevelt in March of 1933.

. . . He said that the year 1936 would be the year in which the world started toward World War II. Nineteen thirty-six was the year the League of Nations died, Hitler marched into the Rhineland, Italy invaded Ethiopia, and most of the major powers sent men to the adversaries in the Spanish Civil War.

. . . In August of 1941 Cayce told a young man about to enter the service that he should not expect to get out until 1945, when the World War would end.

. . . In 1939 he said, "A sad experience will be for this land through 'forty-two and 'forty-three." Those were, of course, the worst years of the Second World War for the United States.

. . . In June of 1938, Cayce, talking about domestic matters, said, "a new order of conditions is to arise. There must be greater consideration of the individual so that each soul becomes his brother's keeper. Then certain circumstances will come about in political, economic and whole relationship in which a levelling will occur or a greater comprehension for the need for it. The time or period draws near for such changes. It behooves all who have an ideal—individuals, groups, societies—to practice faithfully the application of this ideal."

Lyndon Johnson's Great Society made that prediction come true.

. . . In the 1920's Cayce, who knew nothing about real estate, advised friends to buy land north of Virginia Beach. At the time the valuable land in the area was to the south. Those who followed his advice and bought in the north became wealthy.

. . . In 1932 Cayce predicted that by 1962 the Norfolk, Newport News-Hampton port would be the chief seaport on the East Coast.

By 1964 this was a reality.

In 1932 Cayce, warning about physical changes in the world in the years 1958 and 1959, said, "There will be upheavals in the Arctic and Antarctic that will make for the eruption of volcanoes in the Torrid area: and there will be then the shifting of the poles so that where there has been a frigid or semi-tropical climate there will be a more tropical one, and moss and fern will grow."

Late in 1960 a second active volcano was found in the Antarctic and in 1963 a volcanic island appeared off Iceland.

. . . On June 20, 1943 Cayce, speaking of the war, said, "On Friday next, strange things will happen which will determine how long, how many and what will be necessary." On June 25, the Germans and the Russians fought what has been called the greatest tank battle in history. This battle is hardly remembered today, but at least one historian said that Heinrich Himmler recognized the Germans' defeat in the battle as the conclusive sign that the war was lost and that the Germans must then plan how to save face and future.

This is an impressive collection of predictions, but there is little of the supernatural about them, and by themselves they would not have won Cayce the followers he did win during his lifetime and has won since. These people were either doctors whom he had helped to save lives or effect cures, or people he had helped directly with his readings.

At a "reading" Cayce would lose consciousness. Then a trusted associate, usually his wife or secretary, would give him the name and address of the person seeking help. Here are just a few of the cases that defy explanation:

. . . Aime Dietrich, the five-year old daughter of C. H. Dietrich, a prominent citizen in Hopkinsville, Kentucky, had never recovered from an attack of grippe at the age of two. After the attack, her mind had stopped developing. Many specialists had examined her and had agreed that her brain suffered irreparable damage. After hypnotizing himself Cayce said, "The trouble is in the spine. A few days before her illness, the body slipped while getting out of a carriage and struck the base of the spine on the carriage step. This injury caused a weakness where the grippe germs could settle and cause both the mental conditions and later attacks." Then he described the treatments the little girl would need.

. . . A few days later Dietrich phoned Cayce and between sobs told him the little girl had called her parents by name for the first time in three years. Two months later she started school with children her own age.

. . . During a reading for a railroad executive named Andrews, Cayce said that "clary water" should be used in the treatments. No one in Kentucky recognized the term. Andrews inserted advertisements in medical journals that asked for information about "clary water." When no information was forthcoming, Cayce went into a trance and gave the formula for making clary water. While a druggist was mixing it, a letter arrived from a man in Paris. The writer's father had developed and sold clary water but had not sold any for fifty years. The writer attached the original prescription which was identical to the one given by Cayce while he was in a trance.

. . . When Carrie House, wife of Tom House, a friend of Cayce's, became suddenly ill, her doctors said she had a tumor and needed immediate surgery. She refused to give permission for the operation until she had a reading by Cayce.

Cayce said Carrie's illness was traceable to a stoppage of the bowels and her pregnancy. The specialist on the case was scornful, but conceded that the treatment the mystic prescribed could do no harm. After the diagnosis proved to be correct and the treatment efficacious, House told his friend he was sorry the second part wasn't true, because Carrie could not bear children. Carrie proved Cayce right again when she presented House with a daughter seven months later.

. . . A four-year-old child was having trouble breathing. The doctors agreed she had an obstruction in her windpipe, but X-rays had shown no trace of foreign matter therein. Cayce said the obstruction was a celluloid collar button and told where it rested in the windpipe. The amazed doctors removed the button which, because of its color, had not appeared on the X-rays, and the child's health was restored.

. . . An Italian consul who had heard about Cayce from a friend wrote asking for a reading. When Cayce went into his trance and started the reading, he spoke perfect Italian. This would happen many times with many languages.

. . . In one reading Cayce prescribed a certain medicine no one was familiar with—as in the clary water case. A second reading revealed that a drug store in Ohio had one bottle of the mixture. When contacted, the Ohio druggist replied that the last bottle had been sold some time back. A third reading said there was still one bottle left and pinpointed its location. The incredulous druggist looked and found the bottle hidden behind a new line of mixtures he had just brought into the store.

. . . In a similar case Edgar suggested that the supplicant, a lady, use "codiron." Again there was general bewilderment, as no medicine of that name could be found.

Cayce had another reading and gave the name of the Chicago firm that marketed "codiron." When contacted, the firm sent a bottle but asked, "How on earth did you learn of codiron? It is a brand-new product just perfected. We selected the name only a few days ago and have not even made an announcement of it."

. . . Shortly after an osteopath named Frank Dobbins started to practice on Staten Island in New York, he was visited by a woman who said she had been searching for him for some time. Dobbins had been hard to locate, because he was so new in the community his phone wasn't listed. The woman said that her daughter needed treatment outlined by Edgar Cayce in a reading, and that Cayce had said, "Find Dobbins. He can do the job."

Dobbins had never heard of Cayce until that moment, but after he followed the instruction and cured the child, he became a friend and follower of the mystic's. Later he moved his practice to New York City, where he spread the word that he indeed depended on Edgar Cayce for help.

. . . One day Cayce's boy Hugh Lynn dropped a match into a pile of flash powder and burned his face severely. When the eye doctors said they had to remove one eye immediately, Cayce said they could do nothing until he gave a reading on it.

He also insisted that the doctors be in the room when he had the reading so that they could help with the prescribed treatments. When he awoke the doctors were disturbed because he had recommended that Hugh Lynn be kept in a dark room for fifteen days, with bandages soaked in tannic acid that were to be changed frequently, kept on his eyes.

The doctors cooperated and Hugh Lynn made a complete recovery.

. . . Once when facing one of his constant financial crises, Cayce read on the problem of housing for his family. When his son asked where they should live Cayce said they should "buy the house across the lake," and that although they had no money the payments would be made.

On Friday, the day the down payment was due, Cayce was broke. But the owner of the house phoned and said he couldn't meet with him until Monday. On Monday a check for $500, the needed amount, arrived at Cayce's office.

. . . Nineteen years after Cayce's death Alan Hovhaness, a half-cripple, was transmogrified into a healthy, exuberant man by a series of exercises devised by Cayce years ago.

. . . Today several hundred doctors and osteopaths are studying Cayce's readings because they are convinced that he was, as one doctor said, "a generation ahead of his time." While asleep, Cayce was a human medical library, and in his readings he covered everything from halitosis (he was certainly a generation before television) to serums for cancer that haven't been mixed yet.

Because of his record Cayce's predictions about our immediate future deserve our attention. Our lives may well be affected by them.

In these predictions he has said that—

. . . By 2100 New York will have been destroyed by either an atomic attack or by earthquake.

. . . Los Angeles and San Francisco will have been destroyed before New York.

. . . Part of Alabama will be covered by water.

. . . A good part of Japan will have slipped into the ocean.

. . . The continent of Atlantis, which theoretically disappeared into the ocean in 1530 B.C., will rise again.

. . . Communism will end in Russia and that country will become "the hope of the world" as an ally of the United States.

. . . Red China will be Christianized and will become a democracy.

. . . The earth's rotational axis will tilt further, causing a reversal of climates.

Here is the story of that remarkable man whose wonders no one has yet been able to explain or to duplicate. . . .

EDGAR CAYCE
MYSTERY MAN OF MIRACLES

by Joseph Millard

REVISED EDITION

A FAWCETT GOLD MEDAL BOOK

Fawcett Publications, Inc., Greenwich, Conn.

Member of American Book Publishers Council, Inc.

Chapter One

FOR SOME CURIOUS and never-explained reason, farmers in Christian County, Kentucky, always had been plagued by the birth of animal monstrosities. A normal sow would farrow piglets with two tails or a split snout or missing ears. A cow would calve a horror with two heads. In one grand orgy of deviation, prankish nature delivered to a shocked farmer the only seven-legged calf on record.

In the years afterward a great many people were firmly convinced that the greatest freak of nature ever spawned in Christian County was the baby boy born to young Leslie B. Cayce and his wife that March afternoon in 1877. The proud parents named him Edgar, after one of Leslie's brothers. He looked like any normal, healthy, homely, newborn boy, and yelled just as loudly.

The country thereabouts was so full of Cayces that it was claimed nobody could keep track of them all, not even Grampa Cayce, patriarch of the clan. Even Grandma, his own wife, had come of Cayce stock a few generations back. When news of Leslie's son got out, they came in swarms and droves to see him.

Leslie B., who was just twenty-three, brought out a keg of whisky and a tin cup to pass while he strutted and bragged and took his turn at the cup. "He'll make his mark in the world some day, and you can bet on that. Just listen to him yell. Did you ever hear a stouter pair of lungs at his age?"

There came a night not long afterward when that lungpower went on and on until Leslie's temper was frayed and his wife was on the verge of hysteria. "I don't know what's wrong with the baby," she cried, wringing her hands. "He won't stop crying."

"Well, for God's sake do *something*," Leslie roared, "before this howling sends me out of my mind."

She tried, but nothing seemed to help. Then, about midnight, there was a knock at the door. It was old Emily, a colored woman on the place, puffing her corncob pipe. She said, "Miz Carrie, I been hearin' the baby cry and I thinks I knows the trouble."

"Then tell us," Carrie Cayce said. "I am almost wild."

"We see," the old woman said.

She sat down by the crib, drew hard on her corncob pipe, and then blew a cloud of the fragrant tobacco smoke against the soles of little Edgar's feet. The third time she did this he stopped crying, sighed, and fell asleep. It was the last time the baby ever had an attack of colic.

From the day he took his first toddling step, Edgar revealed a remarkable talent for getting into trouble. It seemed to his distracted parents that every time they took their eyes off him, there would be a crash and a yell to signify another disaster. One afternoon, during a torrential downpour, he managed to push the front door open, crawl through, and fall off the porch. On another occasion he fell into a pond. How he got himself out remained a mystery, for he was much too small to know how to swim.

Finally, in desperation, his father hired an eleven-year-old neighbor boy named Ned to act as daily companion and bodyguard. Thereafter his father could devote more time and attention to his new importance in the community.

Leslie Cayce had been elected justice of the peace, a high honor for one so young. Now he was addressed as Squire Cayce, a title he carried throughout his life. He began to stalk with dignity and to spend more and more time at his brother's crossroads store, talking politics with the men and delivering his opinions in a firm, authoritative voice.

He was never a man given to a show of affection or to any very warm and intimate comradeship with his son. Edgar stood in more than a little awe of the stern head of the family, who had positive, no-nonsense ideas about what constituted right and wrong and who would brook no deviation.

Carrie Cayce was just the opposite. She was a sweet and gentle woman, patient and understanding, with more than a touch of the mystical in her nature. More than anyone else, she understood her son. She cheered him when he was despondent, pointed out the right path when he was confused. Without her wise spiritual guidance, Edgar Cayce's uncanny powers might never have developed, or might have been turned into wasteful or destructive avenues.

Next to his mother, the ones who understood him best and with whom he felt the closest bonds were Grandma and Grampa. In many ways, Grandma was like Carrie Cayce in her sensitivity to feelings and impressions too subtle for the commonplace mind.

Grampa was what some men called out-and-out strange. For one thing, he was a dowser of note in the county. Neighbors were forever coming over to the farm to ask Grampa to find out where to sink a well for the easiest and best water. Sometimes he would take the boy along on these expeditions.

Along the way Grampa would stop and cut a slim fork of witch hazel and trim off the leaves. When he got to the place where a well was wanted, he would grip the two forks of the witch hazel, holding it in front of his chest with the stump of the main branch pointing straight ahead. Then, with Edgar running breathlessly beside him and the men pacing close, he would begin to walk back and forth.

Presently he would cry, "Hold it now, boys. I think I'm beginning to get something."

He would move more slowly and cautiously until Edgar could actually see the witch hazel quivering and jerking downward. Grampa would tell them to dig right there, and invariably the men found good water, close to the surface and in ample supply.

Grampa could do other, even stranger things. One of Edgar's earliest memories was of Grampa putting his fingertips lightly on the top of a heavy table and somehow making that table rise straight up in the air. He would stand and stare at the broom in the corner for a minute and the broom would suddenly stand up straight and dance around the room with no one even near it.

These things both fascinated and frightened Edgar. "How do you do it, Grampa?" he would cry. "What makes it happen? Could I do it if you showed me how?"

"I don't know what the power is, boy," Grampa would say, "but don't fool with it."

In his younger days Grampa had sometimes done tricks like that at parties. Gradually he grew more reluctant until at last, while Edgar was still very young, he stopped altogether. "Whatever it is that does those things is something too big to just be frittered away on idle amusement. I don't know why the power was given to me but I'll not mock it again."

Shortly after this pronouncement, he was killed before Edgar's young and uncomprehending eyes.

It was the June following the boy's fourth birthday, and the two had ridden out to look over some field work. Grampa was in the saddle on his big horse, with Edgar bouncing behind, clinging tightly to his belt the way he always rode. On the way back to the big house they passed a deep pond. The sun was hot and Edgar's pants were soaked with the horse's sweaty lather.

"I'm going to let him drink from the pond," Grampa said. "You'd best get down and wait in the shade, boy. He gets a mite skittish sometimes in the water."

Edgar slid down and watched Grampa ride the horse out beyond the cattails and lily pads to the clear water. The horse arched his neck and sucked noisily.

Suddenly something, a frog or turtle or perhaps his own rippling reflection, frightened the animal. He reared up high, squealing and lashing the water with his front hoofs, then spun around and lunged for the shore. Grampa kept his seat, sawing at the reins and calling, "Whoa, boy! Whoa, boy! Steady!"

The horse whirled on his hind legs and crashed back

14

into the pond. Trembling with fright, Edgar saw the horse stumble and jerk forward with such force that the saddle girth snapped. Grampa and the saddle were hurled over the animal's head and into the water. The horse, even more terrified, reared up again and brought his hoofs down on the very spot where Grampa lay. Then he wheeled and went galloping away with reins flying.

Edgar ran down to the edge of the pond and called to Grampa as loudly as he could. There was no answer, but he could see a shapeless something out there under the ripples and a redness beginning to tint the water. He knew something was terribly wrong. He began to cry and ran home as fast as he could.

The next day he watched weeping relatives gather around a big box in the parlor and tried to understand what it meant when they told him Grampa was dead. The only part that was clear was that Grampa wouldn't be keeping his promise to take Edgar hunting in the fall and let him shoot a real gun for the first time.

It was months before Grampa came back and explained about having to break that promise.

After the funeral Grandma was lonely in the big house, so Leslie and his family moved in with her. Edgar liked that, because he could talk to Grandma about things no one else but his mother understood. The squire had taken over the crossroads store, and Carrie Cayce was busy supplying Edgar with baby sisters at minimum intervals. Still, she found time to talk to him and encourage his dreams.

He was growing into a grave, skinny, intense little boy who would rather creep into a corner and listen to mantalk than go romping noisily with children his own age. Somebody remarked that he was more like a little old man than a child, and some of the relatives took to calling him Old Man instead of Eddie.

The squire made valiant efforts to talk to his son, but he usually ended up baffled by the strange things the boy would say or ask. "That kid spends too much time by himself, daydreaming and imagining things," he

15

would tell the crowd around the cracker barrel. "Too much of that will make any boy queer in the head after a while. He needs playmates to rough him up and bring him out of himself."

"He don't care none for marbles or any games, that's sure," a man would say. "Now my kids are into some kind of hell-raisin' all the live-long day. Only time they'll set still is when your Eddie gets 'em together and tells 'em stories about places like Egypt and some others I guess he just makes up. I've heard him a time or two and I swear, he tells those things so real you'd think he'd been there and seen 'em himself."

"I know." The squire would nod. "And the funny thing is, I looked up some of the stuff in books, and blamed if he doesn't have it exactly right. How he found out I can't figure, since he can't read. Every once in a while I come on him out in the garden, jabbering away a blue streak all by himself. I ask him who it is he's talking to and he points around as sober as a judge and says, 'Why, I'm talking to my little playmates right over there.' It like to give me the creeps sometimes."

Those incidents bothered Edgar, too, at first. He wondered if his father and most other people had something wrong with their eyes when they couldn't see the little boys and girls who came to play with him. His mother saw them sometimes, and he had a feeling Grandma could, too, if she tried.

They were children his own age, and they came from somewhere every day, but only when he was alone. When anyone else came near, they simply vanished. Sometimes they played active games, but often they just sat and told one another stories. Then, when he began to understand why others could never see his friends, they told him he was getting too big for them to visit anymore, and they went away.

He was out playing around the tobacco barns one day when a familiar voice said, "Hello there, Old Man."

He turned and there was Grampa, smiling at him just the way he used to. The only difference was that Grampa's body didn't seem to be quite solid. They talked for a long time, the way they used to before the accident.

Grampa had been looking over the tobacco crop, he said, and he explained to Edgar about not being able to take him hunting. After that Grampa came quite often and they had wonderful long talks together. He told Grandma and his mother about the visit, and neither of them seemed surprised. But something inside warned him that it might be better not to confide in the squire.

It was about this time that an old colored woodchopper on the place sat down for twenty minutes and changed the whole course of Edgar Cayce's life.

He told the boy a Bible story with all the drama and intensity a Negro can pour into his living religion. Edgar sat enthralled. To him it was the most wonderful and exciting story he had ever heard. When it ended, he ran to his mother.

"The Bible is full of stories like that," she told him. "If you like them so much, I'll read or tell you many more." Thereafter, whenever she was not occupied with nursing babies, she read him the old stories. He loved them all and believed every word without question. "I want to learn to read," he told her passionately. "Then I'll read the whole Bible for myself."

"Keep doing that," she told him, "and you'll never be alone and never be misled."

On a night of wild excitement, the big house caught fire and burned to the ground. No one was hurt, but the family had to divide up and stay with various relatives until it could be rebuilt. Edgar went to stay with an aunt who was much like the squire in many ways.

In a misguided moment of confidence, Edgar told her about his phantom playmates and about the visits with Grampa. She was outraged. "Eddie Cayce, don't you know it's plain wicked to let your imagination run away with you and make you tell stories that aren't true? Shame on you. You know very well dead people don't come back and talk to little boys."

"I don't see what's wicked," Edgar said. "It's true. Mother sees my little friends and she'd see Grampa too, I know, if she happened to be around when he comes."

"Your mother!" his aunt said, tight-lipped. "This is all her doing and I'm going to speak to her firmly about humoring you in such tomfoolery. She'll have you completely addled."

He never knew exactly how his mother handled the situation, but he knew better than ever again to tell such experiences to other people. He was beginning to sense the fact that he and his mother and his grandmother dwelt in a world apart, separated from others by some strange, invisible gulf.

At his aunt's he missed his mother's daily Bible readings, but there was an exciting substitute. She had a huge family Bible, so big he could scarcely lift it, crammed with thrilling illustrations by Doré. He could sit for hours, looking at the pictures and telling himself the wonderful stories.

That winter, when he was seven, he got his chance to learn to read.

Chapter Two

HIS AUNT took in a boarder, a beautiful young woman called Mrs. Ellison. She was a devout Mormon, a former schoolteacher who was said to have been one of the wives of Brigham Young before polygamy was outlawed. When the shock of this wore off, the parents of the community took up a subscription and hired her to open a school. Aunt Ella let her use a room in the house for classes, and here Edgar had his first head-on collision with Love and the ABC's.

The love was a schoolboy's first crush on a charming and sympathetic teacher, and under its spell the first capsules of learning slid down without a struggle. Mrs. Ellison discovered the boy's passionate interest in the Bible and fanned that interest with her own zeal. After classes and in the evenings she would read Bible stories to him and engage him in long, earnest discussions of the meaning of verses. It was Edgar's first introduction to theology, and he could never get enough of it.

"I'm going to be a minister," he told her earnestly, "and tell people all about the Bible. Only I'd like to be a doctor, too, so I could make all the sick people well. I wish I could be both."

"You can," she told him. "There are medical missionaries who go to far countries and heal the sick bodies at the same time as they save heathen souls."

"Then that's what I want to be," Edgar said positively.

By spring he could read well enough to stumble through some of the Bible stories for himself. Mrs. Ellison closed her school and moved on to some better opportunity, but the seeds she had planted in the boy's mind were rooted and sprouting. The goal of healing both bodies and souls obsessed him. A dozen times a day he would slip away into the woods to pray for its realization.

He had no intimate friends his own age, no interest in the games they played. The closest contact he had with some of them was through his fists. The violent, explosive temper that would plague him all his life could be triggered by any junior Doubting Thomas.

Edgar had a firm and simple conviction that everything in the Bible was literally true and remained unchanged over the centuries. The miracles of old were still possible if you had faith, and his faith was unshakable.

"Aw, that was a long time ago," some boy would argue. "Anybody knows there ain't any miracles anymore. You can pray yourself black in the face, Eddie Cayce, but you'll never make any blind men see or lame men walk. You can't do it."

"I can so do it," Edgar would yell and charge in with fists swinging to prove his point.

School, under a succession of teachers, male and female, was a greater tussle for the gangling, moody boy. Without the encouragement and charm of Mrs. Ellison, Edgar made rapid strides toward setting the Christian County record for inattention. He began to feel more at home in the dunce's corner than at his own seat. It was not that he was either dull or rebellious; he simply could not refrain from drifting off into his own dream world, remote from the classroom and its problems. Reading was the only subject in which he showed progress, because every moment of spare time was spent reading his mother's Bible.

This, at least, met the squire's wholehearted approval. At last he brought Edgar a Bible of his own. Edgar never forgot that memorable day—January 14, 1887, two months short of his tenth birthday.

The family was back together again after the dispersal. A fine new house had been finished for Grandma. The squire's many brothers had pitched in to help build him a smaller house in the woods close by the big one.

One of the results of this reunion was that Edgar began going to church with the family. What was an ordeal to most of the other boys was a source of endless delight to him. This was the Christian Church which, with the Campbellites, had branched off from the Presbyterian Church, and was as stoutly fundamentalist as the hardest hardshell Baptists.

About this time he conceived the project of reading his Bible completely through at least once for every year of his life. At the beginning he had a tendency to skip over the endless "begats," but in time he began to be interested in even the lineage of his heroes. By his thirteenth birthday he had caught up and was well launched on his thirteenth reading. It never grew dull to him, for each new reading opened new vistas of thought and revealed exciting new points that had eluded him before.

With implicit faith, he prayed every day for the power to heal, and never doubted for a moment that his prayers would be answered. In this his mother concurred. *Ask and it shall be given. Seek and ye shall find.* These were statements, clear and unequivocal, and she held to an unshakable conviction that one day the truth of them would be manifested in her son.

But while he dwelt much of his time in a spiritual world, Edgar was also living a thoroughly normal physical exsitence and finding it rugged. During one of the periodic teacher shortages, the squire himself took over the school and had a close-range opportunity to see his son's peculiarities and shortcomings.

Patience had never been one of Leslie Cayce's virtues. The clashes that developed over his son's wool-gathering in the classroom were frequent and violent. It seemed to the boy that the harder he tried to learn lessons and keep his attention on books, the farther afield his mind would wander.

Presently the squire turned the school over to a brother, Julian, with a grim admonition. "I don't know what's wrong with that son of mine, but you see to it that he learns his lessons, even if you have to beat them into his head." Uncle Julian did his best to oblige.

One Sunday Edgar came home from church particularly stirred by the day's message. He slipped off into the woods, and spent the afternoon reading his Bible and praying for the chance to heal the sick. His mind was still full of the fervor when he went to bed that night.

Some time after midnight he became aware that the room was suffused with a strange radiance brighter than the light of the full moon. He sat up sharply and saw a figure standing at the foot of his bed. It was a woman, and he thought first it was his mother. He started to speak and the figure seemed to melt away.

Edgar jumped out of bed and ran to his mother's room. His first thought was that someone was ill and she needed him. Both his mother and father were sound asleep and the babies were quiet. He went back to his bed, trembling, not knowing what he had seen but frightened by it.

As he lay down, the radiance returned, growing brighter until it paled the moonlight. Suddenly the figure was back again. It was a woman, and on her back were curving shadow shapes, like the angels' wings in the Bible pictures. He tried to speak but his mouth was dry, his breath locked with fright.

The woman smiled. "Don't be afraid. Thy prayers are heard. You will have your wish if you will remain faithful. Be true to yourself. Help the sick, the afflicted."

The light faded and she was gone. Edgar ran outside into the moonlit yard and fell on his knees to give thanks for the vision and the promise.

After breakfast the next morning he drew his mother aside and told her what had happened.

She hugged him joyfully. "I knew you were meant for a great work, son. I've always felt God has set you apart for a purpose. But do try harder to study your books and not upset your father."

That day he was so filled with the wonder of his vision that books and Uncle Julian might as well not have existed. For the other students, the day was enlivened by even more clashes than usual, climaxed by a long session after school. When Edgar was finally released,

Uncle Julian stamped to the store to talk the matter over with the squire.

"I hate to say this, Leslie, but I'm coming to the opinion that boy of yours is plain stupid in the head. He either won't learn, or he can't. Today he sat through the whole study time and never took his eyes off his spelling lesson. Well sir, I thought this time he'd know it for sure so I asked him to spell 'cabin.' Cabin—a simple little word like that. Do you know, he just sat there with his mouth open and didn't even know how to start it."

"Cabin," the squire said. "Cabin!"

"I lost my temper," Julian said. "When I'd my say, I made him stay after school and write 'cabin' on the blackboard five hundred times. He did it without a whimper, but I vow if I were to ask him right now, he couldn't spell it."

"He'll know by tomorrow," the squire said through set teeth. "You did just right, Julian, but I'll promise to do better."

There was a violent scene at home. The squire was a proud man and the knowledge that his only son was talked about as little better than an idiot cut him to the quick. Edgar was slammed into a chair and the drilling begun.

Over and over the squire spelled the words in the lesson. "Cabin. C-a-b-i-n. Spell it."

"Cabin," Edgar would say earnestly. "C-a-b-i-n."

They would take two more words, then, "Now spell 'cabin.' "

"Cabin," Edgar would say blankly, "K . . ."

The back of the squire's hand knocked him clear out of his chair. It didn't, however, knock any knowledge of spelling into the boy's head. After three grueling and painful hours, "cabin" was still one of life's darker mysteries to Edgar, as were all the other mysterious words in the lesson.

At last, reduced to a state of strangled impotence, Squire Cayce stormed out to the kitchen for a drink to cool his rage. Edgar leaned his head back, exhausted by his ordeal. He closed his eyes and a woman's voice sounded clearly in his ears.

"Why do you struggle so? You have our promise. Sleep a few minutes and give us a chance to help you."

The boy thought, Sleep! I will sleep a little, and felt his consciousness slipping away into soothing, dark shadows.

The squire stamped back from the kitchen and glared at the drowsing figure. He gave the skinny shoulder a violent shake.

"Wake up, Edgar, you dummy. Go on to bed. You're just stupid, and it's hopeless to try to beat any knowledge into your head."

"Wait," Edgar cried anxiously. "I just needed to sleep a few minutes. Ask me the lessons again. I know the words, now."

Snorting, the squire barked a word, and Edgar spelled it instantly and perfectly. He went on to spell every word in the lesson, then every word in the book, including future lessons not yet studied. In a burst of confidence, he told his father which page each word was on and described the pictures on that page, for his mind showed him each page complete, exactly as if he were viewing the book itself. He felt very proud of his newly acquired ability.

"So," the squire roared at last and hurled the spelling book across the room. "You knew your lessons the whole time. You just acted dumb to plague and torment your uncle and me." *WHACK!*

Edgar picked himself off the floor and scuttled for his bed.

It was upsetting to discover that knowledge, no matter how perfect, is not necessarily a guarantee of easier existence.

Chapter Three

THE SPELLING EXHIBITION Edgar staged in class the next day nearly broke up the school. For him to spell three words of a lesson correctly would have been startling; to have him stand up and calmly score a hundred per cent created a small sensation.

His classmates gaped and Uncle Julian pounced on him, sure that his nephew was cheating by reading from hidden notes. Edgar let him finish his futile search and then explained the mechanics of his miracle. When he demonstrated his new ability by reeling off the lessons not yet reached by the class, Julian Cayce was forced to surrender to a mystery beyond his comprehension.

"All I can say is, you'd better sleep on the rest of your books, then. You're as big a dunce as ever in geography and arithmetic."

Edgar followed the suggestion and became the Eighth Wonder of the local world. Julian reluctantly promoted him to the next grade and went to discuss the situation with his brother. "It just isn't natural for that boy to know everything in the books, Leslie. I'm not even sure it's proper to advance him when he admits he doesn't study, but on the other hand I can't hold him back when he does know all the answers."

The squire was in no mood to quibble over technicalities. From shame over his dullard son, he had swung around to a vast and vociferous pride. "Never you mind *how* my boy does it, Julian. He does it, and that's enough. At the rate he's going, I expect he'll be the smartest man in the country before long."

Edgar's new-found talent brought other changes into his life. His classmates had always considered him an

25

odd fish. Now they considered him an odder fish than ever, but a fascinating one. He suddenly found himself the center of awed attention. At recess and after school they crowded around him to beg, "Hey, tell us again how you learned the books, Eddie. Can you show us how to learn our lessons by sleeping?"

This sudden popularity was thrilling. When they began to drag him into their games, he made a valiant effort to play, although he had little knack and even less experience. During one of their recess games a few days later, Edgar blundered into the way of a hard-thrown baseball and was struck on the spine.

He picked himself up, apparently unhurt, but during the remainder of the day's classes he began to show a startling change. He had always been quiet and reserved. That afternoon he became noisy and quarrelsome, talking loudly and throwing things until the whole school was in an uproar. On the way home he grew even wilder. Yelling and giggling, he climbed trees, rolled in mud, and ran out in the road to stop passing teams, nearly causing a couple of runaways.

At home he picked on his sisters and frightened his mother by his crazy antics. She had a pan of coffee beans roasting on the stove. He snatched this, ran outside and planted the beans around the yard. The squire got home, saw that something was wrong and put the boy to bed. Edgar struggled briefly and then drifted into a coma.

Suddenly he began to speak, his voice clear and authoritative. "I've had a shock from a baseball that struck my spine. The way to bring me out of it safely is to make a special poultice and put it at the base of my brain." He named specific herbs that were to be mixed with chopped raw onions for the poultice. When his parents stood motionless, gaping at him, he barked, "Hurry and get on with it if you don't want permanent damage to the brain."

When the poultice was applied, he fell into a deep normal sleep. In the morning he was completely recovered. The squire went to the store, shaking his head.

"That son of mine! I guess there isn't anything he can't do when he's asleep."

The accident had one curious aftermath. For some weeks afterward, Edgar's personality showed a complete reversal. Where he had always been a recluse by preference, he suddenly became violently gregarious. He shunned solitude as fiercely as he had always sought it.

It was during that period that the advance wagon came through, plastering every fence and barn with posters for the John Robinson Circus. There were excited meetings among the boys. Many of them, including Edgar's neighbors, were absolutely forbidden to attend such a sinful spectacle.

"I'm going," Edgar told the boys flatly.

"Gee, Eddie, are you sure your father'll let you? I always thought the squire was set against such wickedness."

"He's going to be away on a business trip," Edgar said, "so I don't have to ask him."

On circus day he saddled his pony and rode off without even a word to his mother. Riding past the crossroads store he was hailed by old Mr. Carter, one of the wealthiest men in the county and a pillar of the church. He stared in horror when Edgar told his destination.

"Eddie, I'm shocked at you, a fine Christian lad who loves his Bible. What would your dear mother say if she knew you were throwing yourself among evil companions, gazing upon brazen females clad in tights? Don't do it, my boy, I beg of you."

"I'm going," Edgar said, and kicked his pony's flanks.

"Wait, boy," the old man called. "The circus costs fifty cents. I'll give you a dollar to abandon this folly and turn back to your home."

Edgar rode on without bothering to answer. He had gone perhaps a mile beyond the crossroads when his pony began to limp. The limp grew steadily worse until the animal was almost falling at every step. Edgar got down, examined the hoof and found a sharp stone wedged in the frog. He pried this out and remounted but the limp continued, worse than ever.

27

He stopped and considered. It was still several miles to the circus grounds and the pony was obviously too lame to be ridden. When he tried to walk and lead his mount, their progress was so slow that he saw that he could never reach the circus in time. Angry and disappointed, he turned and started the long trudge back home.

Immediately the limp disappeared. He mounted and the pony broke into an eager trot. He reined around and started back toward the circus. The pony limped and stumbled.

Edgar reined in and sat for a long time, staring off into space. At last he lifted his eyes upward. "Thank you, God," he murmured. He turned the pony around, and it trotted smartly on the road back home.

That night Edgar was his old self in every way. He sat and talked to his mother, played with his sisters, read his Bible and spent a long time in prayer and meditation before going to bed. The next day he had no interest at all in his former companions, their games or conspiracies. After school he slipped away to be alone under his favorite tree in the woods.

The brief, unnatural fling at defiance had run its course, it would return at odd times in the future to baffle and bother him, and it would be many years before he began to understand the inner conflicts responsible.

That spring of 1893 he was sixteen and man-grown, though still spindly in body. He had completed all the schooling that was offered, so he took a job on the farm of another uncle close by. He rather enjoyed this. The work was not hard and he enjoyed the solitude, the chance to watch and listen to the birds and the small creatures. As time went on he became more and more convinced that he could understand their language and could project his thoughts and feelings to them. Certainly they would come to him and hover close without a sign of fear.

But in another of the curious conflicting facets of Edgar Cayce's nature, in spite of his love for birds, he enjoyed hunting and had achieved some reputation as a guide to visiting sportsmen. He carried a tiny mark on his face, memento of a hunter's stray pellet of birdshot. It bothered the man who had shot it far more than it ever bothered Edgar.

On the eighth of that August Grandma died quietly and willingly, smiling at the prospect of being reunited with Grampa. In her last days she had some serious talks with Edgar.

"You're different from other boys in strange ways, Edgar—ways I don't rightly understand, myself. You have gifts that are not given lightly. For one thing, you have second sight. Few others could see and talk to Grampa or those little playmates you used to tell me about. I don't know the purpose of these gifts, and you don't either, as yet, but you can be sure there is one. God doesn't hand such things out willy-nilly. Don't ever abuse the gifts or treat them lightly. Hunt for that purpose inside yourself in prayer. When you find it, be true to it. And don't ever feel ashamed that you are different from others."

Edgar held her wrinkled hand, and said nothing of a rebellion growing in his breast. More than anything else he had a sudden passionate desire to be normal, not different.

It was important for a new reason. Young Edgar Cayce had discovered girls. Rather, he had discovered *a* girl. She was the daughter of a neighbor, a vivacious coquette who enjoyed being the belle of every party. When he finally gathered enough courage to ask for a date, he was stunned at her ready acceptance. By the time he had squired her to two or three sociables, he was convinced that theirs was the love of all time.

He gathered the nerve to speak his feelings at last, but was quickly disabused. The object of his passion made it very clear that she had no intention of giving up gaiety to be the stodgy wife of a preacher or missionary, and most especially not with a boy the countryside considered a little queer in the head.

Edgar was badly broken up for a time and through with girls forever. A few nights later he had a strange and vivid dream. He was walking hand in hand with a

29

girl. Her face was hidden from him by a veil, but he knew they were deeply in love. After a time they met a strange, winged figure who threw a cloth of gold over their clasped hands and told them, "Together you can accomplish anything; apart you can do little."

They crossed a stream and a muddy road and came to a steep cliff whose top was lost in clouds far above them. Edgar found a sharp knife and began cutting hand- and footholds up the face of the cliff, pulling the girl up behind him as he climbed. They were still climbing, the top still hidden above them, when he awoke.

The dream was so real and disturbing that he was sure it must have meaning. He told his mother, who suggested an obvious interpretation.

"The girl is your real mate, who will walk with you through your life. She is veiled in the dream because you haven't seen her yet, though she is already with you in spirit. The cloth of gold must be the marriage that binds you together, and climbing the cliff by your own efforts represents the life work you will do to support your family."

"It sounds all right," Edgar admitted. "But I'm through with girls."

His mother only smiled and touched her slim fingers to his cheek. It was a dream that would recur more than fifty times during his life. With the passing years he would find himself and his companion climbing steadily higher until, in the last dreams of his life, he could see almost over the top of the cliff. But even after he had met and married Gertrude, the face of his dream-mate remained hidden. Perhaps the veil was finally lifted when he drifted into his last sleep.

Chapter Four

WITH GRANDMA GONE and the big house standing empty, the squire felt rootless and restless. Farming had never really appealed to him the way it did to his brothers. In January of '99 he moved his family to Hopkinsville and began selling insurance.

Edgar stayed behind; the thought of a job in some cramped office or factory made him shudder. On the farm he was close to nature, with the freedom and the solitude he needed to expand his thoughts and dreams, and to search for answers to the things that bothered him.

Grandma had told him he was different from other boys, and he had come to realize that this was so. She had told him to look for the purpose within himself and in prayer. He searched long and earnestly, but he found no answer. His ambition was still to be a preacher and beyond the fact that he could learn sermons in his sleep, there seemed to be no use for his curious talents. What he did need far worse than any gift of second sight was the money for special schooling. That was a problem that bothered him all summer.

On August 8th, the anniversary of his grandmother's death, he was working a span of mules in the field when he felt a presence behind him. He turned quickly and saw only the empty field, but suddenly he knew the woman of his earlier vision was there.

Her voice sounded in his ears. "Quit the farm and go to town. Your mother misses you and needs you. Go to her at once."

The feeling of her presence faded and was gone. Trembling, Edgar unhitched the mules and headed back to the barns. At the announcement that he was leaving, his uncle exploded. "Of all the ungrateful pups! I kept you through the winter and now, with the harvest beginning and help short, you stroll off and leave me in the lurch. Well, I'll tell you one thing. If you're so all-fired anxious to get to town, you'll walk it. I'm not taking time off to drive you."

Edgar rolled up his few belongings and set out to hike the fourteen miles to Hopkinsville. It was late afternoon, but by walking fast and taking short cuts he reached the family house on West Seventh Street in the early evening. The family was at dinner and his uncle was with them, looking sheepish.

"I was sorry I blew up at you, Eddie, so I hitched up a team and took after you. I must have missed you when you took one of the short cuts."

His mother hugged him and cried a little, the girls swarmed on him, squealing their delight, and the squire pumped his hand. In the first flush of reunion with his family, Edgar forgot how the town made him feel stifled and lost among strangers.

The feeling came back the next morning, a Saturday, when he started out to hunt for a job. As he tramped the streets, a sense of hopelessness came over him. His vision had brought him here and dumped him without a hint of a purpose or a plan. That earlier promise that he would serve the Lord and heal the sick seemed remote and impossible.

Thompson's Hardware had no job open. He stumbled out of the crowded tangle, feeling only relief. Next door was Hopper's Book Store. The elder Hopper, who had sent Edgar the Bible years before, had died and left the store to his sons, Will and Harry.

Edgar stepped inside and a warm feeling of belonging swept over him. This was the first place in town where he felt comfortable and at home. He identified himself to the Hopper brothers, telling them about the Bible their father had given him. "I like your store and I want to work here."

"But we don't need a clerk," Will said. "The place is

small. Harry and I do everything that's needed and still have time on our hands."

"I can find things to do. I just want to be here."

"We can't pay wages," Harry said. "There's barely enough business to support the two of us, son."

Edgar started to turn away and then stopped. "Let me work for you here, anyhow. If I can't find ways to make myself worth money to you, I won't ask for a cent. If I can, will you pay me what you feel you can afford or I've earned?"

"Well-l-l," Will said, "that's fair enough, if you want to take the risk."

Edgar started Monday morning on one of the happiest periods of his life. By the end of a week there was no question of his value to the store. The first month the brothers paid him with a new suit. Thereafter, he drew a regular wage.

Outside the store he was still walking a lonely road, with no real friends. His social life consisted of church and Sunday School and evenings at the Sam Jones Tabernacle, where he heard a succession of great evangelists. Besides Sam P. Jones, who had built the huge barnlike hall, he listened to the inspired preaching of such greats as George B. Pentacost, George Stewart, and Dwight L. Moody.

He met Dwight Moody personally and had a long talk with the famous evangelist. When Edgar told of his longing to be a minister and the insurmountable problem of financing the additional schooling it would require, Moody offered some sound advice. "If the Lord meant you to be a preacher, the way will open for you somehow. But don't forget that it isn't necessary to have a pulpit to serve God. Serve Him where you are, wherever you are, and with what you have."

"But I still want to be a preacher," Edgar said.

Edgar had become friendly with a young fellow named Ralph who attended the revival meetings. Ralph lived five miles out in the country and rode horseback both ways each night. After one revival, they stayed on, talking, until midnight.

"You don't want that long ride home in the dark," Edgar said. "Come home with me and stay the night."

Edgar had been growing moody and nervous of late, and on this night the preaching had stirred him to a high pitch of excitement. When they reached home, he found the house overflowing with Cayces from down-country who had dropped in for an unannounced visit. Even his own bed was full and a place had been fixed for him on the narrow couch in the parlor.

"I'm sorry," the squire said, "but your friend will have to ride on home or find other accommodations."

Edgar's brittle temper exploded. "If Ralph goes out tonight, I go too, and I'm not coming back. It's a fine thing when I can't put up a friend in my own home."

The squire roared back and Edgar's mother stepped in to soothe them with quiet words. In the uproar, Ralph slipped out and headed for home. Still seething, Edgar threw himself down on the couch without even removing his jacket or shoes. . . .

Some time after midnight he awoke abruptly to find the entire couch in flames, the room thick with smoke. He sprang up with a yell of alarm, caught up the burning couch and carried it out the front door. A bank of fresh snow quickly extinguished the flames.

His yell had awakened the household, but by the time they got out, the fire was over. Strangely, there was no damage at all in the house and not a burn on Edgar's flesh, though his new suit was burned through in a dozen places. There was no apparent reason why the fire should start in the couch. Edgar had not been smoking and the stove was across the room.

The next day he was in the grip of another of his curious changes of personality, marked by the same frenzied, unnatural yearning for wild company. That evening, instead of going home to supper and then to the Tabernacle, he went straight to the pool hall and began making friends with the crowd that hung out there. He quickly learned the game and was ready as any of them to bet on his skill.

The next morning his second brief revolt against his own nature was at an end. Or perhaps it had merely been channeled into a new direction. That day he became abruptly aware of the number of pretty girls who passed on the street, or came to the shop for books and stationery. After supper he took special pains to polish his shoes and brush his hair. On the way to the Tabernacle he took back streets to avoid the haunts of his recent companions.

At the revival, he gave more attention to the girls in the audience than to the preaching. It was the first interest he had felt in the opposite sex since his painful jilting. Afterward he lay awake for a long time, thinking of the veiled girl who had walked beside him in the dream.

A day or two later a girl named Ethel Duke, a schoolteacher and former neighbor from the country, drove around to the book store. "I heard you were working here, Edgar, and came by to say hello. I want you to meet my cousin, Gertrude Evans."

Edgar looked past her at the other girl in the buggy and a tingling shock touched his nerves. Gertrude was small and delicate and lovely, with dark brown hair and big brown eyes in a sweet face. When she looked at him gravely, acknowledging the introduction, he thought he had never seen a girl so beautiful. The touch of her hand lingered hauntingly in his palm.

"I'm—uh—glad to meet you," he mumbled, feeling suddenly gawkish and uncouth.

"There's to be a lawn party at Gertrude's Friday night. Why don't you come, Edgar? We'd love to have you and you'd meet a lot of nice young people you ought to know."

Gertrude was studying him soberly. "Please do," she said.

"I'd like it," Edgar managed.

"Good. Eight o'clock, then. Gertrude lives on the old Salter place, east of town, just before you get to the Western State Hospital. Don't be late, now."

Edgar stood and watched the buggy out of sight, finding a sudden tightness in his throat.

The days until Friday were nerve-wracking. Edgar was torn between feverish anticipation and quaking fright. The more he heard about Gertrude's family, the more terrified he became.

Her father had been a prominent architect until his death. Her mother was the former Elizabeth Salter, daughter of one of the most prominent families and a reigning queen in society. They lived now in the fine family home with Gertrude's two aunts and her brothers, Hugh and Lynn.

Edgar looked at himself, gangling and awkward in his one suit, a poor farm boy with a minimum of education and no training for the future. His fifteen dollars a month from the book store would scarcely buy one dress for Gertrude. He pictured himself stumbling among the cool, educated, amused guests at the party, uncouth and tongue-tied, and cold perspiration broke out on his forehead.

Only his aching desire to see Gertrude again kept him from sending excuses and fleeing back to the safety of the farm.

That night he had the dream again. The girl was still veiled, but this time he chopped frantically at the rock and struggled much further up the cliff before he awoke. It seemed like a good omen.

He walked the mile and a half to the party with lagging steps, fighting the panic that threatened to overwhelm him. At the edge of the lantern-lit lawn he almost turned and ran, but Ethel Duke spied him and he was trapped. He spent the next few minutes being introduced and mentally kicking himself for his completely unnecessary fears.

Everyone from Mrs. Evans to the last guest was warm and friendly. No one was kind or patronizing, no one appeared to notice his cheap suit or make him feel anything but welcome. In no time he was completely relaxed and chatting as easily as any of them.

Then suddenly he was face to face with Gertrude, and tongue-tied only because his heart was pounding so crazily that his breath locked in his throat. She was dressed in white, with a red rose in her hair. Edgar was sure no angel in heaven could be half so lovely, half so charming.

36

"I'm glad you're here," Gertrude said, and meant it. She laid a hand on his arm and her touch made him tremble. "Since I've greeted everyone and done my duty, I'm free for a moment. Let's walk out here where we can see the moon rise. I can ask you all manner of questions about yourself and what you want to be and everything. I like to know all about people."

His confidence rushed back and he found himself talking easily and without restraint. He discovered with increasing delight that they had many interests in common.

Gertrude loved books and book stores. She, too, was an ardent Bible reader and properly awed by his record in that field. She didn't think Edgar was illiterate at all, despite his brief schooling, and pointed out that book learning was by no means the criterion of a man's character or worth to the world.

Suddenly Gertrude cried, "Oh, my goodness, the party's over and everyone is getting ready to leave. I don't know how the time got by so fast."

In a burst of courage, Edgar blurted, "Could—could I see you again soon? Maybe even call on you?"

Her small hand lingered in his. Her dark eyes smiled in the moonlight.

"I surely hope you do, Edgar, and I hope it will be real soon."

He went down the road on feet that seemed scarcely to touch the ground. Quite suddenly the advice of Dwight Moody came back to him, rich with new meaning. He could never ask Gertrude to wait out the long, empty years it would take him to realize his dream of becoming a minister. Even after he had patiently saved enough money, there would be high school, then college, then Bible school.

But then Dwight Moody had said, "Don't forget it isn't necessary to have a pulpit to serve God. Serve him where you are, with what you have."

He could still serve God at church and Sunday School and in his own life while he was forging the material success to support Gertrude and a family. There was not the slightest doubt in his mind that when the face behind the veil in his dream was revealed it would surely be Gertrude's.

Chapter Five

ALMOST MIRACULOUSLY, on the heels of Edgar's decision not to become a minister, he was asked to teach a Sunday School class. In no time his deep knowledge of the Bible and his flair for telling the old stories with dramatic realism made it the most popular class in town. As the word spread, young people began coming from other churches until his class numbered thirty-eight, the largest in Hopkinsville. To prevent any conflict among churches, he made this a nonsectarian class that met in a different church each Sunday. He was immensely proud, but no prouder than Gertrude, of his mounting reputation as a Bible authority.

But to Edgar, the greatest miracle of all was the casual manner in which Gertrude's family accepted him and his courtship. No one called him aside to ask sternly about his intentions or his prospects. No one pointed out any difference in wealth or education or social position.

As his confidence grew, he finally steeled himself to confess to Gertrude that part of his life that set him apart from others. Trembling and fearful, he told her about his childhood playmates whom only his mother could see, about his talks with a grandfather long dead, and his dreams and visions and the strange power to absorb books in his sleep.

He finished in an agony of apprehension. "Do—do you think I'm queer or touched in the head?"

"Certainly not," she cried, her eyes flashing with indignation. "I think it's wonderful, and your grandmother was absolutely right. You were given special gifts for a special purpose and you mustn't ever stop searching and praying to discover that purpose."

He wanted to kiss her, but he restrained the urge until a few nights later when she accepted his proposal of marriage. Afterward she told him that her whole family had not only approved but confessed they had begun to worry a little because it was taking Edgar so long to speak out. He had never believed such happiness possible.

"I'm going to work twice as hard and save every penny," he shouted joyously, hugging her. "In no time I'll have enough money so we can be married."

He then rushed out and spent all his savings, along with a good slice of his future income, on a beautiful diamond. He compounded his profligacy by shipping it abroad to be cut and mounted.

At this point, he lost his job.

Harry Hopper sold his share of the book store to a new man who planned to take over the activities that had become Edgar's. There was no longer need for a clerk.

Edgar was stunned at the magnitude of the calamity. From the day he first saw Gertrude he had been dreaming of eventually buying the book store and establishing himself as a modest magnate of commerce. No other type of work appealed to him.

The job he finally landed came to him by sheer accident. Wandering the streets, he saw a crowd going into Richards' Department Store and followed it in. The focus of interest was a big sale in the shoe department. Walking around, he encountered a lady he knew who wanted a particular style of shoe. Edgar had just seen shoes of that style on the shelf. To be obliging he brought them to her and helped her find the right fit.

When she handed him the money, he hurried over and gave it to the cashier. Before he could turn away, another woman was tugging at his sleeve, asking him to find something special. He was too polite to refuse.

Just then the manager cornered him. "Young man, who hired you to work in my shoe department?"

"Nobody," Edgar said. "But people kept asking me where they could find special shoes and I found them and they paid me. But I gave all the money I took in to that woman over there. . . ."

"I know you did," the manager said. "I've been watching you, and you know more about our stock than these dolts I'm paying. If you're looking for a job, report tomorrow morning."

Edgar stayed in Richards' shoe department for eighteen months. He was never happy, but he paid off the ring and added a few spare dollars to the savings. To his amazement, Gertrude and her family urged him to quit. In the end it was his mother who forced his decision.

"I've held you by my apron strings long enough," she told him. "I know you're not happy and that you can't see a future in the shoe department job. You and Gertrude need money so you can be married. Get out of Hopkinsville, son. Go where there is the opportunity to do what you like. There are book stores in Bowling Green and cities nearby. I won't hold you back."

With this encouragement, Edgar set his sights high. One of the largest book and stationery firms in the country was John P. Morton & Co., of St. Louis. He wrote for a job and a copy of their catalog. The huge catalog came promptly, but a curt note informed him there were no jobs open.

He set his jaw and tramped around to call on every businessman in Hopkinsville. Through the book store and his Sunday School class, Edgar was well known and liked and every man was happy to write him a glowing letter of recommendation. He began bombarding Morton's with this ammunition, sending a new batch of letters with every mail. Within a week he got a telegram:

STOP SENDING RECOMMENDATIONS AND REPORT FOR WORK.

He kissed Gertrude and his family good-bye and set off with high hopes. The last thing he did before leaving was to put himself to sleep with his cheek on the fat Morton catalog.

After a week on the new job he was completely accepted by both the management and his fellow clerks. His intimate knowledge of the entire catalog was a source of endless wonder. Almost immediately he was given the first of several raises, and he wrote Gertrude that their future was assured.

He plunged into Christian Endeavor work and joined a group called the Glad Helpers Society. Once a week they visited the prison and the city hospital to sing hymns, read the Bible, and discuss religion with the inmates.

He was getting along fine and well pleased with his prospects until the approach of Christmas, 1899, caused him to take stock of his situation. The result was a distinct shock. He was making good wages, the best of his life, but he had less money in his pocket than when he made fifteen dollars a month back at Hopper's Book Store.

The trouble was that Edgar had a taste for the best of everything in food, lodging, and clothes. With every raise in pay he raised his standard of living. No matter how hard he tried to discipline himself he was forever yielding to impulse and buying something that wiped out his gain.

About this time he got a letter from his father. "I have a new line of fraternal insurance that's so cheap no member of the order can afford to refuse it. I've sold everybody around Hopkinsville and they want me to spread out and cover the rest of the towns and settlements in this section. I'd like to, but my other insurance is booming right now and I can't get away. If you were home now, I'd make you a full partner in my business and give you the whole fraternal line to handle. You can easily make a lot more money than you'll ever make there."

Edgar was strongly tempted. Besides the prospect of more money, he could work close to home and have at least his weekends with Gertrude. He would also be far removed from the expensive temptations of the city stores and restaurants.

The Morton Company crystallized his decision for him. When he asked for time off to go home for Christmas, he was refused. It was against company policy to give any employee more than Christmas Day. Edgar promptly resigned. They were genuinely sorry to lose him and offered him a proposition. Morton's would pay him a small salary to carry their line of office books and stationery along with his insurance. He accepted with delight and took the next train to Hopkinsville to tell Gertrude that now the world was truly their oyster.

He went on road trips shortly after the new year of 1900 came in, and from the first week prosperity rode with him.

"You're doing wonderfully and I'm happy," Gertrude told him one night near the end of February, "but one thing bothers me. You never say anything about those strange gifts or powers you have. You used to worry so about finding out God's purpose in giving them to you. Do you ever think about that question anymore, Edgar? Do you ever search inside yourself or pray for guidance to help you use the gifts you have as they were meant to be used?"

"Not lately," Edgar confessed. "I guess I'm just too busy making money, Gertrude. When I've saved enough so we can marry and have our own home, then I'll go back to searching."

A few days later he lost his voice.

After leaving Gertrude that night, he began to get a blinding headache. During the next few days the headaches became so frequent and agonizing that he could barely make his calls. He considered giving up and going home, but that would have meant a sharp drop in his week's income, and he was grimly determined that nothing would interfere with his obsession for piling up money.

In Elkton, a busy town some forty miles from home, Edgar finally visited a doctor. He could find nothing physically responsible and merely gave him a sedative powder.

43

Edgar gulped it down and everything went black. When his senses cleared and he opened his eyes, it was to a staggering shock. He was lying in his own bed in Hopkinsville. His mother stood by the bed, weeping, and two doctors were talking gravely to the squire.

Edgar struggled to a sitting position. "What happened to me? How did I get here?" His voice was no more than a hoarse croak, and each word rasped his throat like a burr.

They told him as much as anyone knew. A neighbor, in Elkton on business, had come upon him stumbling around in the cold with no hat and with his overcoat hanging open. His eyes were glazed, his speech incoherent. He stared at the neighbor without recognition, though he allowed himself to be brought home.

The doctors could find nothing organically wrong and concluded that his nervous system had been shocked by too strong a sedative. They left a gargle to clear up the throat condition "induced by chill and exposure while wandering around with his coat open and no hat on."

Edgar gargled faithfully, and every day his voice grew weaker. By the end of March he could make no sound above a faint whisper.

The first time he saw Gertrude after his strange attack, she threw herself into his arms, sobbing. "Oh, Edgar, I'm so afraid. Remember our last evening together? You said you were too busy making money to think about how God wants you to use your special gifts. Right after that you complained of a headache, though you'd never had one before. From then on, the harder you tried to make money, the worse your headache became until this awful thing happened to you. I'm so terribly frightened. I just know this is a punishment or a warning because you turned from your purpose."

Edgar held her close and tried to soothe her. "It's only a temporary attack, dear—the sedative and now the cold in my throat. When it clears, I'll go back to work and make up for lost time. Didn't Dr. Moody tell me anybody could serve God in his daily life without giving up his work to be a minister or a missionary?"

"But you aren't just *anybody*," she wailed. "You're

Edgar Cayce and you have something very special that nobody else in the world has been given. You can't expect to live by the same rules as ordinary people."

He changed the subject then, but afterward, lying in his bed, her fears came back and communicated themselves to him. He pushed them back and clenched his fists, thinking, I've just as much right to happiness as any man. I'm not harming anyone by making myself a good honest living and giving Gertrude a nice home and things to make her comfortable. I mean to do it before anything else.

But a salesman can't sell without his voice. The days slid into weeks, the weeks into months, and there was no improvement. A dozen doctors examined him and spoke learnedly of aphonia and nerve centers and the curious manifestations of hysteria.

It took Edgar a long time to realize that what they were really saying, behind the spate of big words, was that his voice was gone forever. And that as long as he lived, he would never speak above a painful whisper.

Chapter Six

DAZED AND BEWILDERED, Edgar stumbled through a shadowland of horror. He would be in the world but not a part of it. Never again could he lead a Sunday School, preach a lay sermon, or join in discussions. There were only the most menial jobs open to a man without a voice. Even the long, intimate, comforting talks with his mother were ended forever.

Worst of all was his conviction that he must release Gertrude from her marriage promise. She could never find happiness with a voiceless husband, doomed to a life of silence and poverty.

From anguish and worry, his health began to fail. By fall he weighed scarcely a hundred pounds, and everyone was frantic. He had lost all interest in anything around him and all hope for his own recovery.

Then, out of the darkness of despair, came a ray of light. W. R. Bowles, owner of the local photograph studio, approached him one day. "Eddie, I need an assistant at the studio. You could handle it fine because I'll do the talking with customers. Of course, I can't pay you much while I'm teaching you the business, but you'll be learning something you can follow all your life."

Edgar rushed to Gertrude with the news. She hugged him happily. "It's wonderful, Edgar. We'll have our own photographic studio. You can take the pictures and develop them. I'll talk to the people and do the tinting."

From the day he went to work, he began to put on weight, and people in Hopkinsville commented on what a wonderfully sunny disposition young Cayce had, despite his tragic ailment. Bowles was even more delighted when Edgar revealed an unsuspected talent for the mechanics of photography. His business increased and so did Edgar's small paycheck.

He had never been able to wholly forget Gertrude's frightened conviction that his misfortune had been a warning or a punishment. Now it began to haunt his thoughts in the quiet hours of night when sleep was slow in coming. He began to seek and to pray again for the guidance he had rejected.

Where was the road he was meant to follow? There was little a voiceless man could do. It was obvious he was not meant to be a preacher or even a doctor. His childhood vision had promised him his prayers would be answered, and he had prayed only to help others and to heal the sick. There was little help and no healing in the business of taking studio portraits. Was this, too, a forbidden path that would lead only to greater tragedy? Night after night he prayed and listened, but no answer came.

Gertrude consoled him. "I'm sure that when the time comes, you will know exactly what to do, Edgar. I can't explain it, but I have the strongest feeling that great forces are gathering to accomplish something, and that you will be a part of that accomplishment."

During that winter a hypnotist named Professor Hart brought his act to the local theatre. There was, at this time, a tremendous upsurge of interest in hypnotism, not only as entertainment but as a potential tool of medicine. Many leading doctors were embracing it with enthusiasm. Newspapers and magazines carried long articles on the subject and the new term "suggestive therapeutics" was becoming a household word. Schools sprang up across the country to teach the new science and psychologists showed awakening interest in the field.

Hart, who had read a great deal on his subject, was intrigued by Edgar's condition. Hysterical aphonia, with no apparent contributing cause of disease or damage, should be a natural for hypnosis. It also should be priceless publicity for his show.

He issued a public challenge. He would restore Edgar

Cayce's lost voice for a fee of $200. If he failed, there would be no charge at all.

The idea caught on and Edgar's friends were so enthusiastic that his own dead hopes began to rise again. The squire was dubious until Dr. Brown, who had treated Edgar's throat without success, gave his nod to the experiment. "It can't hurt the boy, Squire, and it's just possible it might help." He volunteered the use of his office for the attempt.

It took a little time for Hart's passes to take effect, but eventually Edgar fell asleep. The hypnotist bent close. "You will tell us your name in a clear, normal voice."

Edgar started to answer in a hoarse croak, paused to clear his throat, and then said loudly and without a trace of huskiness, "Edgar Cayce."

The squire let out a yell of delight; Hart and Dr. Brown beamed at one another. After a few more questions, Hart gave Edgar the suggestion to awaken. When his eyes opened, Hart said, "Well, how do you feel now, boy?"

"About the same as I did before," Edgar answered—in a squeaky whisper.

There was consternation in the little office. Hart paced the floor, scratching his head. At last he snapped his fingers. "I know what's wrong. I should have implanted the posthypnotic suggestion that his voice would still be normal after he came out of hypnosis. If I can try again this afternoon, we've got this thing licked. You both heard him talk out clearly while he was under."

They tried again in the afternoon. Edgar spoke normally in his hypnotic trance and obediently repeated the posthypnotic suggestion. When awakened, his voice was the same painful whisper.

Day after day Hart tried and failed. The local newspaper ran what amounted to a score sheet on the attempts, and the whole town was tense with anticipation. Professor Girao, Dean of Psychology at South Kentucky College, came to watch and take notes. No hypnotist himself, he was increasingly interested in the possibilities of the science in the field of psychology. He finally sent all his notes to Dr. John Quackenboss in New York with a suggestion that here was a fascinating mystery in his field.

Dr. Quackenboss, a leading physician, was an ardent booster of hypnotism. He had performed some startling experiments with patients whose subconscious minds, released by hypnosis, diagnosed their own obscure ailments better than he could by physical examination.

Quackenboss came charging out to Hopkinsville to investigate. Hart had given up and moved on, and Edgar had fallen back into a bleak hopelessness. Hart had left one hint when he departed. "He goes into the first and second stages of hypnotism easily enough, though not as quickly as a good subject should. Everything is fine to that point. But when I try to put him into the third stage, the deep sleep where a subject takes posthypnotic suggestion, he fights it off every time. If you could just get him to that third stage. . . ."

Quackenboss made several attempts and met failure. Edgar talked normally under hypnosis. He whispered again the moment he was awakened. The doctor began to get grim lines around his mouth and a harried expression in his eyes. "I'll get him into that third stage yet," he vowed.

At the next attempt he bent over Edgar and repeated earnestly, "You will go into a deep sleep—a deep, deep sleep. You will go into a deep and total sleep."

Unexpectedly, Edgar obliged. He went into a sleep so deep that no effort to awaken him had any effect. Dr. Quackenboss droned his suggestions, mopped his forehead, and droned again. Edgar's mother and father grew increasingly panicky. Onlookers carried the news outside. The whole town began to seethe with worry.

"Do not be alarmed," Dr. Quackenboss told the squire. "There is no possible danger. All experiments have demonstrated beyond any doubt that when a subject is in sleep too deep to respond to the waking suggestion, he merely sleeps it off and awakens normally in a short time."

Fourteen hours later Dr. Quackenboss was still repeating his suggestions and reassurances—and Edgar was still asleep. The family and Gertrude were in a panic.

Some time after noon the following day Edgar opened his eyes, yawned, stretched, sat up, and asked in a squeaky whisper, "What is everybody so upset about?"

Dr. Quackenboss took the first train back to New York, mumbling disjointedly. Edgar, after more than twenty-four hours of total unconsciousness, learned he had not been cured and relapsed into a state of dreary indifference.

It was then that a small, frail, sickly man by the name of Al Layne entered the picture.

Layne's lifelong ambition to be a doctor had been frustrated by finances and ill health. Sickness had already lost him several jobs. His wife opened a millinery shop in Hopkinsville and began to do well. She hired Edgar's oldest sister, Annie, as her assistant. Al Layne took care of the books and devoted the balance of his time to his first love.

He enrolled for a mail-order course in osteopathy. When the new interest in hypnotism swept the country, he added a course in suggestive therapeutics put out by an enterprising outfit in Missouri. The stories in the Hopkinsville *New Era* about Edgar's unsuccessful hypnotic treatments fascinated him. He began to haunt the shop to pump Annie about all the aspects of her brother's condition and the unsuccessful efforts to hypnotize him.

"I'm just a nobody," he said one day, "but I've got a hunch I know where the trouble lies. It's plain as day if you look for it in the reports. I'd like a chance to try to cure him my way."

Annie carried the word home and the squire roared his outrage. "There'll be no more of this making a spectacle and an experiment out of my son. The whole idea is ridiculous and I'll not permit any more of it."

Edgar's mother agreed. "The boy is worse off now than he was before. He's losing weight and getting listless and pale. All this tampering with his mind may very well drive him insane."

But she told Edgar about Al Layne, and something in

50

her words aroused his hope. He talked to Layne and came back filled with enthusiasm. "Give him one chance, Dad. Everybody says it can't hurt me, and he may have something."

There was reluctant agreement at last, and Layne was allowed to try one experiment in the Cayce parlor on the Sunday afternoon of March 31, 1901. The squire and his wife were present and very nervous. Layne was nervous too, since this was his first major effort.

"It's like this," he explained. "Both the others noticed that it took quite a while for Edgar to go under. Then they said that whenever they tried to put him into the third stage, he seemed to resist them and tried to take over himself. I think that's the whole answer. If he wants to hypnotize himself, I'll let him do it. Maybe we'll get what we're after."

"Well, now," the squire said, "come to think of it, when he slept on his books and learned them, he always put himself into that sleep. And the time he got hit with the baseball and was clean out of his head, he spoke up out of sleep and told us how to fix the poultice that cured him. You may have something."

Edgar spoke up in some surprise. "I always have to put myself to sleep, even for them. I lie there while they make all their passes and nothing happens. So I finally get tired and tell myself to go to sleep, and right away I do."

Layne's eyes shone. "Let's get on with this."

Edgar fell into the lighter sleep quite easily. Then Layne said softly, "Now you will put yourself into the deeper sleep, the full sleep, the deep-trance sleep."

Edgar drew a couple of deep, shuddering breaths and then his whole body relaxed. In a shaky voice Layne droned, "Your unconscious mind is looking into your body. It is looking at your throat. It will tell us what it sees that is wrong with that throat and what can be done to cure the trouble."

After a moment Edgar's voice came, clear and unaffected. "Yes, we can see the body. The trouble we see is a partial paralysis of the vocal cords, due to nerve strain. To remove the condition it is necessary only to suggest that the body increase the circulation to the affected area for a short time."

Layne mopped his forehead and leaned closer. "The circulation to the affected areas will increase and remove the condition."

Immediately the area of Edgar's throat turned a deep pink that darkened rapidly to deep crimson as hypnotic suggestion sent excess blood flowing to that part. After several moments Edgar said, "The condition is cured. Suggest that the circulation return to normal and the body awaken."

After a few moments Edgar's eyes opened. He said, "What happened this ti—" He stopped short, his eyes going wide and incredulous. Then he shouted, "I can talk! I can talk! *I can talk!*"

He leaped from the couch, hugged his mother, slapped the squire's back, pumped the hand of the beaming Layne. His voice was as clear and strong as it had ever been. He shouted until the windows rattled and there was not even a rasp in his throat.

When the tumult subsided, Layne said, "You know, while you were in that trance you talked exactly like a trained physician who was looking right down inside your own throat. I got to thinking about that story your father told of how you could put yourself to sleep and look inside closed books. If you can do that with a book, why can't you do it with someone else's body— like mine, for instance?"

Edgar laughed, partly for the sheer joy of making sounds again. "That's the craziest idea I have heard yet. Why would I want to do that?"

"To find ailments or injuries or sources of infection that doctors might not be able to find by regular examination. There are lots of people like me who have been sick for years, but the doctors can't find out for sure what the cause is. It might not work at all, Edgar, but if it did, just think what a wonderful chance to heal the sick."

To heal the sick! The words of the figure in his boyhood vision ran again in his ears. *Be true to yourself. Help the sick, the afflicted.*

"All right," Edgar said slowly. "If you want to try it, I'm game."

"Good," Layne said excitedly. "I'll come over tomorrow morning. I'll make a good subject because I've been to so many doctors I know all their reports by heart and I can tell right off whether you're hitting the mark or not."

Layne left and Edgar raced out to demonstrate his restored voice to Gertrude. He was still staggered by the enormity of the miracle. A few minutes of hypnotic sleep had lifted him out of the depths of despair and restored him to a world of talk and laughter and song, a world where he could once more hope to realize his dreams.

In the course of the evening, he told Gertrude about the crazy, impossible idea of Layne's. She listened eagerly, eyes shining with excitement.

"Oh, Edgar, it's the most marvelous idea I ever heard. Mr. Layne is a genius to think of it. Maybe this is the answer you have been hunting for, the reason and purpose for those strange gifts you have. Just think, Edgar, what if you could simply go to sleep and tell sick people how to get well. Wouldn't that be wonderful?"

"Oh, Lord, no," Edgar said, aghast. "Folks think I'm some kind of a freak, now. What would they think if I started doing anything as crazy as that?"

Chapter Seven

AL LAYNE poised a pencil above a sheaf of note paper and bent toward the couch where Edgar lay in his deep sleep. When he spoke, his voice was sharp with nervous tension.

"You have in this room the body of Al C. Layne. You will go over this body carefully, noting its condition and especially any parts that are ailing. You will give the cause of such ailments and suggest treatments to bring about a cure." He stopped and sat holding his breath. His hand, holding the pencil, trembled with strain. The results he hoped for were so fantastic that he was afraid to let himself even consider success.

The sleeping Edgar Cayce spoke suddenly and clearly. "Yes, we have the body of Al C. Layne here. We have gone over it carefully. Now, here are the conditions of that body as we find them. . . ." He talked on, crisply, incisively. Layne's pencil flew across the note sheets. One after another the filled sheets fluttered to the floor. . . .

Edgar opened his eyes, blinked, yawned and sat up. He looked anxiously at Layne. "Did you get anything?"

"Anything?" Layne said in an awed voice. "I got everything. There's never been anything like this in the history of the world. You're—you're a phenomenon, Edgar. You described all my symptoms better than I could ever do it myself. You told me exactly what was wrong with me and then gave a detailed course of diet and medicines and treatments to cure me. It's all here on these sheets, just as you gave it. I've got writer's cramp from trying to keep up with you. I had to tell you to slow down once or twice, and you did."

Edgar skimmed over a few of the scrawled sheets and then fell back on the couch, his jaw sagging. "That couldn't have come out of me. A lot of those words I never saw or heard of. I haven't the faintest idea of what they mean or even how to pronounce them."

"You did when you were asleep. Some are medical terms for organs and parts of the body and the rest are drugs and herbs. I know enough medicine to be positive everything you said was exactly right."

"Hey," Edgar stiffened in sudden alarm. "Did you say drugs? Oh, no! Don't you go swallowing a lot of stuff just because I babbled about it in my sleep. For all I'd know, some of those things could be poison."

"Don't worry," Layne smiled. "I know every one and there's not a harmful ingredient in any of them. I'm going right home and start following these instructions today. If it works on me, we'll try it with someone else who's sick."

Layne went to assemble the medicines prescribed by the sleep-voice. Edgar sat on the couch, staring at the wall with glazed eyes. He was stunned and bewildered and frightened—more frightened than he had ever been in his life.

"I don't want to be a phenomenon," he mumbled. All he wanted was to make a good living, marry Gertrude and raise a family, as any normal young man does. At twenty-four he had already waited far too long.

Even Gertrude was dazed by the actuality of what she had suggested. "It's simply too incredible to be true, Edgar. Yet it *is* true, and you proved you could diagnose other people. Then you've finally found the purpose in your life, the reason God gave you special powers."

"I don't know," Edgar said miserably, twisting his hands. "This thing is too fantastic. If I just had a gift for doing an ordinary thing better than anyone else, I might accept it. But this is so completely insane. Why should God pick an uneducated country boy like me and give him a special power nobody else on earth seems to have?"

Gertrude laid a cool, soothing palm over his clenched

55

hands. "Joseph was a carpenter," she reminded him gently, "and the disciples weren't chosen for college degrees or social standing."

Despite her confidence, Edgar continued to be tormented by doubts and fears. The whole idea was so preposterous it outraged reason. He wanted only to take Gertrude and flee far away, to escape this mad nightmare that was distorting his life.

For a week he avoided Layne and buried himself in work at the studio. Then one day Layne bounded in, threw his arms wide and shouted, "Look at me! Just look at me! After one week of the treatments you gave me, I feel better than I have in years. I even look so much better that people stop me on the street to ask what I'm doing for myself."

Edgar blanched. "You're not telling them about me?"

"*Telling* them?" Layne cried. "I'm proclaiming it from the housetops. I've got the whole town talking. If I continue to improve like this, everybody in the county will be swarming in for a psychic diagnosis."

"You've got to stop them," Edgar moaned. "It's all a fake. It even fooled me until I figured it out. I've got a power, all right—the power to read minds when I'm hypnotized, that's all. You know medicine and you know what the doctors say about your stomach trouble. All I did was pick that knowledge out of your mind and say it back to you a little differently. You admitted yourself that most of what I said agreed exactly with what doctors had already told you."

Layne threw back his head and laughed. "You'll have to do a lot better than that, boy. Sure, a lot of what you told me was identical with my reports. The doctors were right as far as they went, but they didn't go far enough. You went on to the basic cause of my trouble, something nobody even suspected. Then you gave the additional medicines and treatments to cure the cause. You didn't get that out of my mind, because it wasn't there. If that's a fake, then tell me what's improved my health a hundred per cent in one week."

"I don't know," Edgar cried wildly. "I don't want to know. Just go away and let me alone. Stop messing up

56

my life." He ran into the darkroom and locked the door.

In two weeks, Layne's miraculous improvement in health was the talk of the town, and Edgar was slinking along back streets to dodge the curious. Layne finally cornered him. "You can't hold back any longer. You've insisted you want to help people find health and happiness. Now you know the way. I'm fitting out a couple of rooms over the hat shop with your name on the door as a psychic diagnostician. We'll charge a reasonable fee for a reading, as I call it. A lot of people who thought their cases were hopeless are just waiting for you to start."

"I can't do it," Edgar groaned. "Curing my own throat and suggesting some treatments for you may be all right. But I can't set myself up as being smarter than the best doctors, just because I talk in my sleep. I can't, and I won't."

He carried his torment to his mother, hoping she would set his mind at rest. She heard him pour out his doubts and fears, then said quietly, "Are you sure this isn't what you were meant to do, son? God has given you a strange power to ease the suffering of others. Isn't this exactly what you have prayed for all your life? And isn't it what you were promised in your vision?"

"I just don't know," he said. "I don't know what's going on or what I say when I'm in that sleep. What if I advise some kind of medicine that kills someone? I'll be a murderer."

"Mr. Layne knows enough about medicine to recognize anything poisonous or harmful. He's a good man, Edgar. He wouldn't let you prescribe anything that would bring harm, I'm sure."

"If he knows," Edgar whispered, chewing his lip. "But he's only a correspondence-school osteopath, and not even licensed for that. He can make mistakes. And what if I tell someone their trouble is one thing when it's really something else a lot more serious. I wouldn't know, and neither would Mr. Layne. A person might believe me and treat some little thing while they're dying of something worse. I'd be as much a murderer then."

His bewilderment and uncertainty communicated itself to Gertrude. "I thought it was so wonderful, this great gift of yours, Edgar, and I was positive this was what you were meant to use for humanity. Now I'm not sure, either. But I can't think God would give such a power and let you use it wrongly."

"How do I know this came from God?" he groaned. "I've prayed for an answer to that and there is none. There are evil forces, too. This could be the Devil's power in disguise, using me as an innocent tool to destroy others." He jumped to his feet, his jaw set with determination. "It's too big a risk, Gertrude. Not just for me, but for others. I'm going back to town now and tell Layne I won't go through with it."

He hurried to town. When Layne answered his knock, Edgar said, "I've made up my mind. I'm not going through with . . ." He broke off in horror.

His voice had faded to a thin, painful whisper.

"I guess you'll be your first patient, Edgar," Layne said. "I'll help you give yourself a treatment in the morning. Then we'll sit down and work out the details on getting the work under way."

Edgar turned and stumbled home, his mind in a turmoil. This could be the sign for which he had prayed so earnestly, the assurance that his feet had been set upon the right path. In his heart he wanted it to be the sign. He wanted to help others, but he wanted to know clearly and positively that what he was doing was right.

Still this dramatic loss of voice when he defied the power could as easily be the Devil's work. His reading of the Bible had instilled a bitter respect for Satan's ingenuity. In a remote corner of his mind a nagging question remained unanswered: If God meant me to heal the sick, why didn't he simply make me a doctor—maybe even a better doctor than any on earth?

Edgar never saw the first patients who came for his psychic diagnosis, nor did he ever know their identities. This was at his own insistence. "It's bad enough having to go through this crazy kind of witch doctor or spiritualist business for people who are sick. If I had to face someone I know, I'd be so embarrassed I couldn't go through with it."

Layne shrugged. "Have it your way. It'll be the results that count. I'll handle appointments and listen to their troubles so I'll know what questions to ask you. Then I'll hustle them in and out again while you're asleep."

"But don't ever hide anything from me," Edgar said, looking hard at Layne. "If I say anything wrong or prescribe anything harmful, I want to know it immediately. If someone does what I recommend and isn't helped, I want to know that, too."

"I promise, Edgar. As for prescribing harmful medicines, I can reassure you on that score. Strong drugs or narcotics can't be bought without a regular doctor's prescription. All I can get are simple herbs and roots and infusions that couldn't possibly hurt anyone. If you call for a drug I can't buy, I'll simply ask for a substitute I can get. You needn't worry."

"Another thing," Edgar said. "People, especially doctors, are going to be saying I'm a fake. If they want to make tests to find out, you let them. Urge them to test me and give them every help you can. If I am a fake, I want to know it fast, before I do something terrible. I almost wish somebody would show me up so I could quit all this and settle down to work. This is making an awful mess of my job with Mr. Bowles at the studio."

Layne chuckled. "My dear boy, with your half of the fees we'll be getting here, you can chuck that studio job and start taking life easy. You can marry Gertrude and live on Easy Street."

"Oh, no," Edgar cried. "I'm not doing this for money. I'm willing to go ahead as long as I'm helping other people, but I won't ever take one penny for it. Just keep your price low and pay all the bills. If anyone needs a reading, as you call it, and doesn't have the money, you see that they get it free. That's all I ask."

"All right," Layne said. He shook his head in bewilderment. "You're so all-fired upset about having people think you're some kind of freak. I guess I better not tell this around or they'll be sure of it."

Twice a day, at ten in the morning and two in the afternoon, Edgar rushed from the studio to the new offices to give readings. He could do two a day without feeling too much strain. In fact, he awoke feeling rested and refreshed, though hungry. Layne took to having crackers and milk ready after each reading. At times when Edgar awoke feeling particularly invigorated, Layne told him he had given unusually clear and detailed readings. This gave Edgar a crumb of comfort by indicating that what he was doing was right.

Gertrude worried about Edgar's health. "I keep wondering if it's good for you to go into those trances all the time. Some say being hypnotized over and over can drive a person out of his mind."

"Sometimes I think I'm already out of my mind," Edgar said. "But Layne swears people are being helped if they follow what I say. Some of them won't do all the things they're supposed to and then complain because they aren't getting well, but I guess that can't be helped. Even doctors run into that trouble all the time. He says some doctors came up and tried to prove I was a fake, but they couldn't. One or two even said it was a miracle and that they'd get readings on some of their patients."

He was in better spirits than at any time since the idea started. Nobody jeered him on the streets and some even stopped to thank or congratulate him. His father had come up to watch a few readings and was now strutting around town, bragging to everyone about his son's healing power. This comforted Edgar. The squire was nobody's fool, and if he suspected anything was being done wrongly while Edgar slept, he would make it known in a hurry.

Perhaps the most reassuring of all was that Gertrude's aunt, Carrie Salter, came to see for herself what was going on up there over the millinery shop. She witnessed some readings and issued her flat pronouncement. "You stop this foolish worrying, Edgar Cayce. What you're using is a gift of God for the benefit of humanity and God'll see that it isn't misused. Just you accept it and quit trying to run away from your destiny. I've checked around, and you haven't made one mistake yet."

"One mistake is all I'll ever get to make," Edgar said, his eyes bleak. "One mistake that kills somebody."

He worried mainly about Layne's status. The little man was happily compounding prescriptions, mixing poultices, massaging muscles and even essaying osteopathic adjustments, all without benefit of a single day in medical school or even a pretense of a license. True, none of Layne's activities could be classified as really dangerous to the patient, but they were highly irregular, if not illegal.

"The legal part bothers me, too," Layne admitted, "and I'm saving every cent to go to medical school, Edgar. But you don't have to worry about what I'm doing. Your readings are so clear and detailed that I couldn't possibly do anything wrong. They're a medical education in themselves. Besides, I help people only when their regular doctors are so stubborn and skeptical that they flatly refuse to follow your treatments. There has to be someone to do that or they've wasted their money."

"I suppose so," Edgar said worriedly and got up from Layne's desk to go back to the studio.

Suddenly there was the pound of heavy feet running up the narrow stairway from the street. A woman burst in, her eyes wild with panic, her face chalk-white. A man staggered behind her, a little girl of perhaps four in his arms. The child was gasping for breath, her face almost purple.

"She's choking to death," the woman cried, wringing her hands. "The doctor says there's an obstruction in her windpipe, but they took X-rays and they don't show anything there."

"For God's sake, save her," the father panted. "I thought this was a fake, but if you can save her I'll believe anything."

Edgar was already racing to the couch in the adjoining room, tearing open his collar as he ran. "Hurry up," he shouted back at Layne. "There isn't a moment to lose."

When he awoke, Layne was staring at him strangely. The couple with the child were gone. Edgar sat up.

61

"Where are they? What did I say? Did I do that little girl any good?"

"We'll know in a few minutes," Layne said. "They tore out of here for the hospital the moment you told them what was wrong. I brought you out of it a little more slowly this time, because you've already given two readings before today and I didn't know how an extra one under pressure like that might affect you."

"What was choking her?" Edgar demanded, "What did I say?"

Before Layne could answer, the father ran in. He seized Edgar's hand and pumped it, while tears poured down his cheeks. "You saved her. You saved her when no one else could."

"But what was strangling her?" Edgar demanded again.

"A celluloid collar button she'd swallowed. That's why it wouldn't show on the X-ray plate. The doctor thought I was crazy coming to you, but he found the button exactly where you said it would be."

Edgar fell back on the couch, trembling. He lifted his eyes to the ceiling, whispering over and over, "Thank you, God. Thank you for that child."

Chapter Eight

THE INCIDENT did much to strengthen Edgar's confidence in the rightness of his uncanny power, but nothing to remove his persistent worries. He knew that he was wielding some kind of enormous force, but he was doing it blindly. He was like a man with his eyes covered, firing a gun into the darkness and praying there would be no innocent bystander in the bullet's path. The thought so frightened him that he would wake up at night drenched with cold sweat, sick and trembling.

He had no way of knowing exactly what came out of his mouth while he was asleep, nor to what use or misuse a listener might put the information. He trusted Al Layne as much as he dared trust anyone under such harrowing circumstances. He trusted Layne as a man of honor. He mistrusted him as a man of sufficient training and knowledge to judge unerringly in every case.

He went on giving readings, but each one shook him with a fresh flood of doubt and terror. The strain began to tell on him. He grew haggard and tense and his temper burst out with increasing frequency. Both Gertrude and his mother worried about him.

"I think you should give this up," Gertrude told him one night. "At least for a while, until you feel better. You're getting to be nothing but skin and bones, Edgar. You're moody and you snap at everybody."

"I'll do it," Edgar said. "I'll tell Layne tomorrow to cancel all appointments for readings until I get myself straightened out. This constant strain is driving me crazy."

Another problem was also eating at his nerves. The readings were taking too big a slice of his time from the studio. There was not nearly enough money in his savings to think of marriage to Gertrude, and no hope for any more in the foreseeable future.

"I'm going to have a talk with Mr. Bowles tomorrow," he said grimly. "If he can't pay me better wages, I'll have to look for another job, even if it means leaving Hopkinsville. I can't expect you to wait forever."

"I would," Gertrude said, and her eyes sparkled with tears. "But I'd hate to."

The thought of leaving Hopkinsville was no longer painful, as long as it meant getting Gertrude with him sooner. Perhaps he was imagining things in his state of nerves, but it seemed to him that whenever he appeared on the street, people stared and whispered and pointed at him. The *New Era* had run some stories on his weird talent. He was beginning to feel like the logical successor to the seven-legged calf. Worse, he was certain that Gertrude's friends pumped her about him and wondered privately if she were a little queer, too, waiting endlessly for an impoverished misfit who might land in jail or in the insane asylum.

"I won't give up the readings forever," he told his mother, "but I won't continue them until I've made sure they're being used properly, with a staff of real doctors to hear every reading. That will take away the curse of queerness from me, too, when I'm recognized by scientists and respected physicians."

His decision made, Edgar slept more soundly that night than he had in months.

When he awoke the next morning, his voice was gone.

Layne obligingly conducted an early-morning hypnotic treatment that quickly restored it to normal. Afterward Edgar sat on the couch and bitterly surveyed his future while Layne chattered volubly about the operations.

"You'd have died laughing," he was chortling, slapping his thigh. "It was the funniest thing that ever happened up here. It was old Henry Simms from out east of town. His young wife was ailing so he came in for a reading on her. Well sir, when I told you to find the body of Mrs. Henry Simms, you came right back with

64

'Which one? We have several here.' The old man turned red as a beet. He finally managed to mumble that he'd been married before he moved here, and this was his fourth wife. The reading came through then without a hitch."

Edgar jumped up and tramped to the door. "Four wives," he snarled, "and I can't even make enough money to marry one." He slammed the door on the startled Layne.

He went straight to Bowles at the studio. The photographer listened and nodded sympathetically. "I know it, Cayce, and I've worried about it with you. It's a crime to make a fine girl wait so long. The trouble is that the business here is only big enough to support one photographer and an assistant. You're as good at the job as I am, if not better, but I simply can't pay more than assistant's wages."

"Then I'll have to find another job," Edgar said.

"Now, maybe not. I've been thinking about something that might be just the ticket. I'll rig you up with a set of spare equipment and furnish the supplies. You can go around to the country schools and churches and take your own pictures on a full-share basis. The harder you work, the more you'll make."

"I'll take it," Edgar said promptly.

Throughout the morning he waited anxiously, half expecting his voice to fade in warning or retaliation. Over and over he whispered pleadingly, "I'm not running away or giving up doing the readings. I'll be out of town only two or three days at a time and I'll be home every weekend."

Perhaps his plea was answered, for his voice remained at normal strength, even when he went to tell Layne of the new arrangement.

Layne was distressed. "If you're gone even part of a week, Edgar, I don't know what we'll do. More and more people are coming in for appointments. Even with two a day I've got readings booked for weeks ahead."

"A lot of them are curiosity seekers," Edgar said.

"You'll have to weed those out. But for people who really need help, I'll find the time somehow."

Layne made doodles on the appointment pad and scowled. "Look, Edgar, why don't you quit being a stubborn goat on this matter of money? If you'd take your half of the fees, you wouldn't have to go wandering around the country trying to earn the money to marry Gertude. Why shouldn't you take it? People have to pay doctors for a diagnosis that may not be right at all. They expect to pay you for one that never fails. You're entitled to it and then some. Be reasonable."

"I'm not a doctor," Edgar said flatly. "This isn't something I studied and paid to learn. God gave me a special gift—if it really is that—so I could help others, not get rich by it. I'd never consider abusing my power by commercializing it."

Layne clutched his head in exasperation. "Blast it, wouldn't you say great preachers and evangelists like Moody and Jones have a special gift from God too? You don't see them getting too persnickety to accept a fair wage for their labors."

"You can argue all you want to," Edgar said. "But it doesn't seem right to me and I won't do it."

Layne could only groan and surrender. "But do me a favor, Edgar. Before you leave town, I'd like to have you give me a kind of special reading. I've got some friends, two well-to-do couples, who'd never believe your readings were anything but a fake. They sneered and scoffed until they made me kind of sore. When they went to Paris for the Exposition, I made them a bet. I said if they'd keep a complete record of everything they did on one day, I'd get a reading and have you tell me the same thing here. Then, if what you said agreed with what they'd written down in Paris, they'd have to admit you're no fake."

Edgar collapsed into the nearest chair. "How could you ever claim anything as crazy and impossible as that?"

Layne stared at Edgar for a long, thoughtful moment. Then he said quietly, "It isn't crazy or impossible. You've done it, Edgar. I didn't want to tell you about this before, because you were working yourself into enough of a stew as it was. You're clairvoyant."

"I'm *what?*"

"Clairvoyant. It simply means you have the psychic power actually to see things that are happening or have happened somewhere else, far away. I suspected you might be, and made some tests during readings. You didn't know it, but you've been giving accurate psychic diagnoses lately on people who aren't even in Hopkinsville at the time."

"You're crazy," Edgar gasped. "Or I'm crazy. Or maybe we're both crazy."

"You started it," Layne said. "One day a woman was late for an appointment. I'd already had you go to sleep and she still hadn't arrived. Suddenly you started right in, as usual. You said, 'Yes, we have the body. She has been delayed talking to a friend but she is on the way now. She is just coming down the street, walking very fast.' The next minute she burst in, all apologies, and you gave the regular reading, but you'd already started to diagnose her trouble before she walked in."

"I can't believe it," Edgar gulped.

"I can show you the readings. After that I experimented by having you diagnose people in the outer office. Then I tried it on people at home and finally on people off in the country or in another town. As long as I told you where they were, you went right ahead without any trouble. You even made little remarks about where they were, exactly as if you were there and seeing the place. So I know you're a genuine clairvoyant, along with everything else."

"Oh, golly," Edgar moaned. "Now I'm even weirder than I thought."

"It's a wonderful talent," Layne said, "with a million uses. Will you let me try to get the reading on the folks in Paris?"

"I suppose so," Edgar said miserably.

A day or so later he submitted dully to the test. Afterward Layne showed him sheet after sheet scrawled full of intimate reports of the supposed activities abroad.

"And it's right, too. I'll bet anything on it. Why, you even ripped off those Frenchy names like a native. Anybody'd swear you lived in Paris."

"I wish I did," Edgar mumbled unhappily. "Anywhere but here in Hopkinsville where they know me."

In due time the couples returned and were confronted with the reading. They glanced over the sheets and were stunned. Not only had Edgar detailed every incident related in their own record, but had added personal items they had forgotten to write down but remembered clearly.

Edgar was vindicated but not comforted. Without realizing it, Layne had unwittingly erected a barrier that would never be wholly removed. Edgar's unending fear of what might go on during the time he was asleep had made him hypersensitive. The revelation that Layne had made tests for clairvoyance without telling him had come as a sickening shock.

The tests were without ulterior motive. But he had not been told. That frightened him more than anything that had happened in months. Something had been done while he was unconscious and without his knowledge or consent. Was there anything else that Layne was still concealing? The question haunted him. Even the most innocent experiment with unknown forces might easily have frightful repercussions. Though Edgar still liked and admired Al Layne, he could never bring himself to trust him completely from that day on.

Out of that unhappy situation, however, came one item of knowledge. He knew now that he could give his psychic diagnoses to any person, anywhere, within at least a few hundred miles. In time he would learn the universal scope of his power, but at the moment this was awesome and frightening enough. From then on he traveled to a bedside to give a reading only when the distracted asker insisted, or when his immediate presence was important to take check readings quickly and verify or correct treatments.

Meanwhile, the new arrangement with Bowles was working out well. He was making a little more money and the change of pace helped him smooth out some of the kinks in his nerves.

Each time he returned to Hopkinsville he gave readings on the more urgent cases Layne had weeded out, flatly rejecting any patients who had trivial ailments or seemed merely curiosity seekers. At first he was nervous about withholding readings from anyone for fear his voice might be taken away again as punishment or warning. But as time went on with no repercussions he began to relax.

"It must be all right to limit my readings to people in real distress," he told Gertrude. "Or else the whole idea of some ruling force or spirit that would take my voice away when I disobeyed was only imagination. Sometimes I think that's all it was, anyhow. The doctors said it was nervous shock that had caused me to lose it the first time. I realize now that every time I've lost it since then was when I was worried and upset and under a terrible strain. As long as I stay relaxed in my mind, I'll bet nothing happens to my voice again."

Gertrude shivered and snuggled closer to his side. "Don't say that, Edgar. I think you are being guided and watched, and it frightens me to think what awful things could happen to you if you begin to feel independent."

The day of the first light snowfall, Edgar took a picture of Fountain Park that turned out to be a photographic masterpiece. His camera caught the powdering of snow on the trees and shrubbery, the play of light and shadow, with a rare and breathtaking beauty. Bowles had it made up into a Christmas card that attracted wide attention. Several thousand were sold and Edgar received a nice bonus.

He was out tramping the woods one day when he heard a distant shout, "Edgar! Edgar Cayce!"

A few moments later Layne came running through the woods, waving a telegram. "Edgar, I just got a wire from a man in Chicago who heard about you and wants an immediate reading on his wife. She's in the hospital in very bad shape. He says it's urgent. Can you come back to town with me and give it this afternoon?"

69

"It it's that urgent," Edgar said, unbuttoning his collar, "we can't take time to go back to town. I'll give the reading right here."

He loosened his shoe laces, lay back on the frosty ground and folded his hands over his solar plexus. In a few moments he was asleep. Layne read off the woman's name and location in the Chicago hospital, but before he could finish the initial suggestion, Edgar began to twitch violently.

"Wait," he shouted. "We have the body and it is in very bad condition. An operation performed a few days ago has just opened up. The body is hemorrhaging internally. Unless this bleeding is halted at once there is no hope of survival."

Layne barked the command to awaken, then started to run. Over his shoulder he yelled, "I'm going to phone the hospital long-distance. Come along when you're ready."

Edgar hurriedly retied his shoe laces and set out for town. He had no idea what he had said during his sleep, but it was obviously a matter of great urgency.

Layne was just hanging up the telephone when Edgar got to the office. Layne's face was gray, his eyes dull. "You said the woman was bleeding to death internally. I got through to the hospital as fast as I could, but it wasn't fast enough. The doctor said she died five minutes ago—from an internal hemorrhage."

The tragic death of the unknown woman upset Edgar badly. For several days he was too stunned to work. Not even the saving of the child with the collar button in her windpipe brought home the enormity of his power so sharply. To Gertrude he moaned over and over, "I could have saved her. If I hadn't been out in the woods—if Layne could have found me in time . . ."

"Stop it," she told him sharply. "Stop blaming yourself. A doctor must learn to accept the fact that he can't save everyone. You must learn that too, Edgar. You have to lead some part of a normal life or you'll tear yourself to pieces."

To get his mind off the tragedy, Gertrude showed him a new puzzle contest being run by a New York newspaper. They began to work on it together, and gradually his spirits lifted and the sense of personal guilt faded away. By the time they sent off the last puzzle, he was quite normal and cheerful again.

A few weeks later he returned from a trip to learn that he had won the contest and a fine gold watch, which he carried with great pride. The Hopkinsville *New Era* ran a story congratulating him on his triumph without mentioning one word of his psychic powers. People stopped him on the street to speak about his good fortune. Edgar began to feel more like a normal member of the human race than he had in years.

He was on the road one day in the spring of 1902 when one of his Hopkinsville friends phoned him. "I can get you a mighty good job if you want it, Edgar. Potter's Book Store in Bowling Green needs an experienced man right away, at a good salary. You're in if you want it."

"I want it," Edgar said happily. "Tell them I'll be there, ready to start work, day after tomorrow."

When he hung up, he felt like dancing. Here was the realization of all his dreams. He could get away from Hopkinsville and Layne forever. In a new town where no one had heard of his psychic talents, he could make genuine friends and lead a normal life at last in the work he loved best. A good salary meant he and Gertrude could be married soon and set up housekeeping far away from the old associations.

He gave scarcely a thought to the possibility of losing his voice as a result of abandoning the readings for a while. He had practically convinced himself that the whole idea was imagination, anyhow.

Edgar canceled all photo sittings and headed back to Hopkinsville in high spirits. Bowles took the news with good grace, though he hated losing him. Layne heard him out in silence, then said quietly, "All right, Edgar. I guess you know best. I'll cancel the readings. If you change your mind . . ."

"I won't," Edgar said, and rushed out to tell Gertrude the big news.

It had been a long time since he had felt so free.

Chapter Nine

EVERYTHING about Bowling Green seemed ideal from the start. He loved the town and its picturesque setting on the river, and Potter's Book Store was like home. He and L. D. Potter took to one another on sight.

He moved into Mrs. Hollins' boarding house, a short walk up State Street from the store. His roommate was Dr. Hugh Beazely, an eye, ear, nose, and throat specialist. Other roomers were Dr. John Blackburn, an M.D.; his brother, Dr. James, a dentist; Robert Holland, a department store clerk; and Joe Darter, a YMCA secretary. They were a lively crowd, none of them much older than Edgar, and they swept him into their circle of activities at once.

Edgar joined the Christian Church and wrote rapturous letters to Gertrude about their future home in Bowling Green. The doubts and fears and worries of the past were fading from his mind like the memory of a nightmare.

Gertrude wrote worriedly about the readings and the responsibility of his psychic power. Was it right simply to abandon a gift that could help so many? Would something happen to him again if he did? He wrote back reassuringly. The young men around him at the boarding house were serving humanity and still leading thoroughly happy, normal lives. Maybe some day, under different conditions, he would resume the psychic diagnoses. Meanwhile he was entitled to live his life, and he meant to do it.

The next day his voice was down to a rasping whisper.

When Layne heard it on the long-distance telephone

he seemed more pleased than surprised. "You'd better grab the night train and get right over here. I'll wait up to conduct the treatment."

On the trip to Hopkinsville, Edgar stared bleakly out the coach window into the darkness. He felt sick and hopeless and more than a little frightened. There was no longer any use in trying to pretend he was a normal human being with a will and freedom of choice. He was not a person at all. He was a puppet controlled by forces beyond human comprehension. When unseen fingers twitched the strings, he must dance whether he wanted to or not.

Twenty minutes after he reached Layne's office he was awake again and his voice was normal. Layne studied him thoughtfully. "I think I ought to keep checking on you every couple of weeks so this doesn't happen again. Suppose I take a ride over to Bowling Green every second Sunday? At the same time, I can let you know if there are any really urgent cases and see if you'd feel like giving a reading."

"All right," Edgar said dully. "But for the love of heaven, don't let anybody over there know about the readings. They've got the idea I'm just an ordinary young fellow like themselves and I want it to stay that way."

In a short time Layne was spending every Sunday in Bowling Green. Whenever they could be alone in Edgar's room for a few minutes, he gave a reading for one of the urgent cases. Layne always seemed to have his pockets full of pleas for help. The rest of the week, Edgar's new life moved so smoothly and pleasantly that he gradually forgot his fears and adjusted himself to the schedule.

One day in late summer Edgar received a long-distance call from C. H. Dietrich, former superintendent of schools in Hopkinsville and one of the town's leading citizens. "Are you familiar with the case of our little daughter, Aime, Mr. Cayce?"

Edgar said he was. Aime Dietrich had been, and still was, a beautiful child. Three years before, at the age of two, she had suffered an attack of grippe. When it cleared up, her mind had simply stopped developing. The finest specialists in the country could offer no hope. The brain, they said, had been irreparably damaged and would never go beyond the two-year-old level. Later, even that small intelligence began to fade away.

"A while ago," Dietrich was explaining, "she began to have convulsions. These have steadily increased in frequency and violence. Doctors give us no hope at all. Then we heard of some miracles you have performed. Mr. Layne assures us that you can save her if anyone can. Will you come and see what you can do? I've already arranged with the railroad to have a paid ticket waiting for you at the station."

"I'll be on the next train," Edgar said instantly. "I don't know what I can do, but I'll try."

Edgar got on the train with no premonition that this step would change the course of his life. The Dietrich case would become a classic and one of the most famous in his career.

Layne was waiting for them at the house, with Mrs. Dietrich and the little girl. Aime looked normal until one saw the vacant dullness in her eyes, the aimless movements of the pudgy hands.

"Do you want to examine her?" Dietrich asked.

"No, no," Edgar said quickly. "It wouldn't mean a thing to me. I don't know the first thing about medicine."

The Dietrichs exchanged shocked, despairing looks.

From the depths of his hypnotic sleep, however, Edgar's voice held a new ring of authority. "The trouble is in the spine. A few days before her illness, the body slipped while getting out of a carriage and struck the base of the spine on the carriage step. This injury caused a weakness where the grippe germs could settle and cause both the mental condition and the later attacks. Now here, as we see it, is the way to remove the condition and restore the body to normal. . . ."

Layne was writing furiously. The Dietrichs were staring with open mouths, an expression of dazed awe on their faces.

When Edgar awoke he saw Mrs. Dietrich weeping, but the radiance on her face made them tears of joy. Dietrich seized his hand. "The first hope we have known in three years. I don't know how you do it, but you've given us hope at last. Nobody could have known about the accident on the carriage step. We'd forgotten it ourselves until you reminded us."

"I'm to make some delicate spinal adjustments," Layne said. "You told me exactly what to do and how, and you said once they were done, she would begin to return to normal."

"You're to stay and take something you called check readings," Mrs. Dietrich added, clasping and unclasping her hands. "You said it might take several tries to get the adjustments exactly right."

Edgar got out as fast as he could and rushed to Gertrude. "I'm scared stiff. I told Layne to monkey with that little girl's spine, but how do I know he has enough knowledge and skill to keep from doing worse harm? This is awful. We'll probably both land in jail and that'll be the end of everything for us."

"You'll do no such thing," Gertrude said sharply. "You'll save that baby and make her well and then no one can ever doubt you again. If that's the last thing you ever do, you will have repaid God for giving you this miraculous power."

The check reading, taken the next morning, said Layne had made only part of the adjustments properly. It gave instructions for another attempt. There was no hint of alarm in the tone of the reading. Layne tried again, with greater confidence. That afternoon a check reading reported almost complete success, but some minor adjustments still needed correcting. Layne was proceeding with extreme caution, fearful of causing added injury.

The third check reading, the following morning, was brief. "Adjustments have now been properly made on all points. Improvement has already begun."

Edgar went back to Bowling Green with the grateful tears of Mrs. Dietrich still damp on his hand. He was staggered by the unqualified faith in the rightness of the readings. I wish I had half as much faith in myself, he thought. Please God, don't let me fail them. Worry rode him night and day.

Five days later Mr. Potter called Edgar to take a long-distance call. He lifted the receiver, sick with fear. Dietrich's voice, choked with emotion, beat against his eardrum. "God bless you, Edgar Cayce. God bless you. Yesterday our baby picked up her old favorite doll and spoke its name. Today she called us by name. Her mind is fairly leaping ahead to catch up with the years she missed. Don't let anyone ever try to tell me there aren't miracles today."

Edgar hung up and leaned against the wall. He was trembling and limp with reaction. The enormity of the force that seemed to be his to command hung over him like the sword of Damocles. It was a responsibility greater than any mortal should be asked to assume.

"And the only time I can use it," he whispered, "is when I'm asleep and have no knowledge or control over what I do."

By November, Aime Dietrich was healthy and normal. She had practically caught up with children her physical age in every respect and was ready to start school with those her age. News of the case had been widely spread by the Dietrichs, their neighbors, and anyone who had known the child before. It created a sensation and was written up in the newspapers, but by a minor miracle the publicity had failed to spotlight Edgar in Bowling Green. There, his life was still as normal as it could ever be, and he was pathetically grateful.

His bank account was growing steadily but not nearly fast enough to marry Gertrude and establish a home. He was looking everywhere for ways to make more money, but he steadfastly refused Layne's pleading that he accept pay for his readings.

About this time he gave one that was to fit another solid rock into the foundation of his mysterious accuracy. Layne had brought him a request for a reading from a man named Andrews, a railroad director. Among the treatments advised was the use of clary water.

"What is clary water?" Layne demanded afterward, scowling at his notes. "I never heard of it and neither has the druggist."

"How would I know?" Edgar asked.

The reading was sent to New York. No one there had heard of clary water, either. Andrews was so convinced of the authority of Edgar's reading that he bought paid advertisements in medical and pharmaceutical trade papers, asking for information on the unknown product.

Meanwhile Layne got an idea. "Let's take another reading and ask your spirit or force or unconscious or whatever to tell us what clary water is or how it's made."

The reading was taken. The response was a completely detailed formula for the preparation. This was rushed to Andrews in New York, who immediately set a druggist to compounding the mixture. Before it could be delivered, Andrews got a response to his advertisements.

A man in Paris, France, wrote that he was not surprised to find that no one knew of clary water. It was a prescription his father had developed and marketed, but had discontinued more than fifty years before. He ended, "I am enclosing a copy of my father's original prescription so that you may have it duplicated if you wish."

The prescription enclosed was an exactly detailed copy of the one Edgar had furnished during his reading. Even Layne was awed by this further evidence of omniscience.

"Andrews is rich, and he wants to pay you almost anything you could ask," he told Edgar. "Furthermore, he'll sing your praises to all his wealthy friends and associates. You'd better stop all this nonsense and accept the fact that you are delivering the goods and entitled to honest pay."

"Never," Edgar said flatly. "I'll never accept a penny of pay for using my gift as it was intended to be used. You may as well stop arguing with me, because I'll never change."

"You're a fool," Layne said bitterly.

Chapter Ten

IT SEEMED TO EDGAR that every time he managed to get himself reasonably adjusted to the fact that he was different from other people, some new aberration would crop up. The latest, and in some respects the most shocking, made its appearance on a late Sunday afternoon in Bowling Green.

Layne had been there for the day, getting readings and reporting triumphs. Edgar was walking back to the depot with him when they met a man tramping down the street, wrapped in a cloud of personal misery. He was a drab, dull, nondescript little man.

As they met, Edgar glanced at him and shuddered. "Ugh! What a horrid combination of colors."

Layne threw a startled glance back, then stared at Edgar. "What colors? I thought he was about as colorless as any man I've ever seen."

"Oh, I didn't mean his clothing," Edgar said. He made a gesture, circling his own face with a forefinger. "I meant the colors that shine out around him. They were a hideous, jarring combination of darks. Didn't you think so?"

Layne stopped short, his mouth open. "Let me get this right. Are you speaking of his *aura?*"

"Aura?" Edgar said blankly. "What is that?"

"Holy Moses," Layne said softly. "An aura is a kind of radiance that mystics and clairvoyants claim they can see shining out around everybody. Do you mean to tell me you could actually see one around him?"

Edgar stared at him in complete bewilderment. "Do you mean other people don't see that glow from everyone? Why . . . I thought everybody saw that, just the way they see a man's ears or his hair."

Layne's eyes had a dazed expression. "Edgar, don't let this upset you, but you're seeing something that only one person in millions dares to even claim he could see. I never saw an aura, and I don't know of anyone else who ever did."

"Oh," Edgar said miserably. "I really am a freak, and that's certain."

Edgar worried for a time, then eventually began to examine the phenomenon more closely. He observed that the shades and colors changed, and in time he came to recognize the reasons why, and learned to judge feelings and emotions and intentions by those colors. Many years later he even wrote a booklet about the subject. But it took a lot of getting used to before he could consider aura dispassionately.

Meanwhile he had come to a decision. The longer his marriage to Gertrude was postponed, the more obstacles would be thrown in its way. The thing to do was forget ambitions and plans for a fat bank account and a fine home and go ahead together on what they had. Gertrude was in wholehearted accord. He could get a pleasant double room at Mrs. McCloskey's, directly across the street, and they could take their meals with Mrs. Hollins. The date was set, the die cast.

They were married in Gertrude's parlor on Wednesday, June 17, 1903, at four-thirty in the afternoon, before a crowd of happily sniffling Cayces and Salters. Reverend Smith from the Christian Church performed the ceremony. Gertrude's brothers, Hugh and Lynn, were ushers. Dr. Hugh Beazely and Bob Holland brought Edgar over from Bowling Green, held him up when his knees wobbled, and kept him from losing the ring.

At Guthrie they were joined for a wedding supper by Tommy Crawford, a friend of Edgar's, and his new bride. In the gaiety of the moment Edgar managed to forget for a little while that it had been more than six weary, frustrating years since their engagement, and he had still achieved no financial security.

It was after ten that evening when the foursome

reached Bowling Green, but the depot platform was crowded. They stepped off the train into a shower of rice and a shrieking pandemonium. More than a hundred young folks from the church and Christian Endeavor were there to greet them.

Gertrude hugged Edgar's arm, her eyes shining. "I ought to feel jealous, darling. You have so many wonderful friends and they seem to love you almost as much as I do."

Edgar grinned and nodded, swallowing a lump in his throat. No one could ever know how much it meant to him to have all these friends, or how frightened he was that he would lose them if they ever found out about his psychic powers.

Edgar and Gertrude were idyllically happy for three days. But on Sunday, when they crossed the street for dinner at Mrs. Hollins', they saw Layne sitting on the porch with the other boarders. Edgar winced, feeling cold terror coil around his happiness. Gertrude gasped and wailed, "Oh, Edgar, can't we have even our first Sunday dinner without him?"

"He won't bother us," he soothed her. "I'm sure he wouldn't have intruded today if someone wasn't in desperate need of a reading. I'll get it over with quickly and send him away."

He spoke with assurance, but he was in a panic. He greeted Layne stiffly. Layne felt it and was plainly nervous as they trooped in for dinner at the big table. There was an extra guest that day, a circuit judge named Roup, who augmented his income by picking up news for the papers. He frowned at Layne when they were introduced. "Layne? Layne? That name is very familiar. I suppose we've met at some time or other when I was in Hopkinsville."

Edgar could feel a cold perspiration on the back of his neck. The others knew Layne only as a friend from Edgar's home town who visited him practically every Sunday. A casual word from Judge Roup could blast everything wide open.

Layne felt the tension and understood the reason for it. In a desperate effort to change the subject, he turned to Edgar and blurted the first thing that came into his mind. "Mrs. Dietrich says to tell you Aime is already at the head of her class in school. The teacher says she's brilliant."

Judge Roup laid down his fork. "Dietrich. Layne. Now I remember. You're that Doctor Layne who treated the Dietrich child with some kind of mumbo-jumbo you got from a crackpot spirit medium."

Layne slammed his knife down and shouted furiously, "Edgar's no crackpot and he's no spirit medium. He's a psychic diagnostician. He's told me how to treat hundreds of patients in the past two years and there hasn't been a single failure."

There was dead silence around the table. Gertrude suddenly muffled a sob, pushed back her chair, and fled. Edgar half rose to follow her, then subsided. They were all staring at him. A cold numbness spread over him.

Layne dropped his head, mumbling, "Gosh, I'm sorry, Edgar."

"I guess it doesn't matter much," Edgar said drearily. "I knew having friends and being treated like a normal human being was too good to last."

They all began to talk at once, firing questions at Edgar. Layne did most of the answering, detailing cases and answering Dr. Hugh Beazely and Dr. John Blackburn in technical medical terms. When they shot questions directly at Edgar he could only gulp and say dismally, "I don't know. I don't even understand those words you're using. Medicine is all Greek to me."

"But how do you do it?" John Blackburn demanded. "Where do you get this information that is supposed to be accurate?"

"I haven't the faintest idea," Edgar admitted.

"I came to get a reading today on a woman who's very sick," Layne said. "If we can use Edgar's old room, you can all watch how it's done and hear the reading for yourselves. There's nothing secret about it, but Edgar hates to have people think he's queer or some kind of freak."

Dr. Beazely jumped up. "Let's go. I want to see this."

When Edgar awoke after the reading they were all

81

staring at him with the look he had come to know so well. He mumbled an apology and went across the street to his room.

Gertrude flew into his arms and clung to him. He buried his face in her hair. "I'm so sorry, dear—so terribly sorry. I thought here in Bowling Green everything would be different. Now that it's out, I might as well pitch a tent in the front yard and charge people a quarter to come in and gape at me."

"I don't care," Gertrude cried fiercely, hugging him. "I'd never be ashamed to have people staring at us because my husband helps others. It's helping others that counts, not how you go about doing it."

Edgar held her close and kissed her tenderly.

Judge Roup's story of Edgar and Layne, including his eyewitness account of the reading, broke on the front page of the Bowling Green paper the next morning. There was quite a stir of interest and curiosity, but the reaction turned out to be not nearly as bad as Edgar's imagination had pictured it. Nevertheless he could sense the old familiar barriers going up as his warmest friends saw him suddenly as someone different, a being set apart.

After dinner the next evening, Dr. John Blackburn drew Edgar aside. "I had quite a talk with your friend Layne yesterday after you left, Edgar."

"You did?" Edgar said. He knew what was coming and a cold chill touched his nerves.

"We can't let this go on, you know," Blackburn continued gently. "Layne is a sincere man and remarkably skilled for one with only correspondence-school training, but he doesn't have nearly the knowledge a doctor must have to treat the public. He has been lucky so far in not making a mistake that could be serious or even fatal. That luck can't hold forever. But even if it did, you can understand that if one amateur is permitted to practice medicine without training and a license, we let down the barriers for a horde of crooks, quacks, and bunglers."

"I know," Edgar said miserably. "That's been my greatest worry. What are you going to do?"

"The only thing I can do," Blackburn said. "Turn Layne in to the Medical Association."

Two Sundays later Layne arrived in Bowling Green, had a short talk with Edgar, and left without waiting for dinner. Edgar raced across to the room where Gertrude waited. He bounded in, swept her up in his arms, and pirouetted around the room, shouting, "We're free! We're free!"

"You ninny," Gertrude cried, laughing and struggling. "Let me down and explain what you're yelling about."

Edgar laughed joyously. "I can't give any more readings because the Medical Association has put Layne out of business. They closed his office yesterday."

Gertrude's smile faded. "What are they going to do to him? And what about you? Will you be in trouble, too?"

"Not with a friend like John Blackburn. He persuaded the Medical Association not to prefer charges or hand out any punishment. In fact, they helped Layne enroll in the Southern School of Osteopathy so he can get his license. He's leaving tomorrow, and that means we're free. No more readings, and no more worries."

The affair was not to terminate quite that smoothly. The newspapers picked up the account of the Medical Association's action and published a story that was more colorful than accurate. A few people interpreted his connection with Edgar as some kind of sinister conspiracy to hoodwink the public. But his greatest shock was a summons to appear before the Board of the Christian Church to be examined on his fitness to continue in the congregation. He told them his story, withstood a severe cross-questioning on his morals and religious beliefs, and so confounded them with his knowledge of the Bible that they voted to let him remain a church member. He went home, thankful but badly shaken by the experience.

"But it's all over now," he told Gertrude, holding her close. "They finally had to believe me, but they all seemed a little bit relieved when I said I wouldn't be able to continue with the readings now that Layne is gone."

"If you're happy," Gertrude whispered, "then I am,

83

too. But I hate to think of people who might suffer or die when one of your readings might make them well."

"Don't think about it anymore. Remember what you told me: a doctor has to learn that he can't save everyone."

The next morning Edgar's voice was only a thin whisper.

He left Gertrude in tears and went to John Blackburn. "If you can't find a medicine or treatment that will help, I'll just have to take the train down to where Layne is. I can't sell books without a voice."

"Layne told me about your peculiar aphonia and how you finally cured it yourself. Look, Edgar, you hypnotize yourself, so all you actually need is someone to give the suggestion and then tell you to wake up. Why couldn't I do that for you right here?"

"Would you?" Edgar squeaked incredulously. "But I always had a feeling that you never quite accepted this business, that you had a suspicion in the back of your mind that somehow it was fishy."

Blackburn swung around and stared out his office window. After a moment he said quietly, "Maybe that's why I'm particularly anxious to try it for myself. That is, if you want me to."

"Which couch?" Edgar whispered, loosening his tie.

When he awoke, his voice was normal. Blackburn was staring at him with dazed incredulity. "I saw it happen. I don't even want to believe it, but I have to because I saw it. I told your bloodstream what to do, and it obeyed."

"I wouldn't believe it either," Edgar said, tying his shoes, "except that it always brings my voice back. Isn't it awful to have to go through life knowing you're some kind of freak?"

"Awful?" Blackburn said. He sprang up and paced the floor, smashing a fist into his palm. "It's tremendous. I'm convinced now it's the greatest power on earth. All the years of training of all the doctors in my graduating class put together aren't a hill of beans toward helping humanity compared to what you can do in your sleep. This can't be stifled, Edgar, but it can't be allowed to run wild, either. Your power must be controlled and used."

"It looks like I haven't any choice," Edgar said morosely, "if I want to keep on talking out loud."

"Let me study this. I'll figure out a sound procedure and we'll get started right away."

"All right," Edgar said. If he had to go on being a one-ring circus, it was comforting to know that he had at least one believer with a medical license. . . .

The next day Blackburn brought his plan. "I talked it over with Hugh Beazely and went to some of the biggest doctors in town. They're all interested and willing to form a committee to give this thing a thorough scientific investigation. We want to study your power, find out how infallible it really is, and then harness it to do the most good."

Edgar hurried home to Gertrude, feeling a vast weight lifted from his shoulders. "I never wanted to stop using my power to help others. It was just that I was always afraid of making a terrible mistake with no one but Layne to check what I said. Now I won't have to be afraid anymore, with trained doctors to see that my readings can't hurt anyone."

Gertrude hugged him, her face radiant. "Oh, I'm so glad, Edgar—so terribly glad. I've wanted you to use your gift as it was meant to be used, too, but I felt the same as you did about trusting Mr. Layne's knowledge too far."

With the weight of doubt and fear and guilt lifted from his mind, Edgar was like a new person. He went down several times to visit Layne at his college and report on the new developments. Thanks to the knowledge gained from Edgar's readings, Layne had been permitted to start as a second-year student and was progressing swiftly toward his coveted degree.

"Blackburn conducted a reading for his committee of doctors," Edgar told him. "They were pretty badly shaken by the whole thing, but I think they're convinced now that whatever my power is, it isn't a fake. With a group like that on my side, I don't feel quite so much like an odd fish anymore."

He was getting considerable publicity now, but it was less of the sideshow oddity type and more tinged with respect. On one of his visits to the Southern School of Osteopathy he confounded the professors as well as the students by giving perfect diagnoses of their most difficult cases. A number of professors and scientists heard of Edgar Cayce, came to witness readings and make tests, then went away to write baffled and contradictory stories about him.

Meanwhile there was still no solution to Edgar's eternal problem of money. His pay at the book store had reached its peak and was still insufficient. He finally settled everything by leaving the store. In partnership with Frank Potter, a relative of the book dealer, he bought out a photographic studio on State Street. A side room was furnished with a couch. Here Edgar gave his readings, and here Blackburn and the rest of the committee of doctors liked to gather evenings to discuss tests and experiments.

The evening of New Year's Day, 1906, Blackburn dropped over. He knew Gertrude was in Hopkinsville for the holidays, so he suspected Edgar would be at the studio. He tramped up the stairs and opened the door. The small room seemed to be full of doctors. At his entrance they turned and stared at him silently, their faces haggard and drawn.

Blackburn stopped short. "What is it? Is anything wrong?"

"Hell, yes! Edgar Cayce's dead."

Chapter Eleven

FROM THE DAY he opened the State Street studio, Edgar had driven himself like a man obsessed. From early morning until late at night he was arranging, snapping, developing, then charging out to sell some more profitable deal.

He had always had a horror of debt. Gertrude had made the studio possible by persuading him to accept a loan from her aunt, Carrie Salter, to uphold his share of the partnership. This debt haunted Edgar, and he was grimly determined to pay it off above everything else. Equally frenzied was his desire to lift Gertrude out of the monotony of a dull furnished room into a house of her own. He longed to sit down to a dinner table covered with snowy linen, before a crackling fire, with a servant or two to serve the most elegant courses on the finest china.

These dreams drove him to a fury of effort; the studio prospered. Gertrude filled in as receptionist and they added two young men, Tom Barnes and Frank Porter, as studio assistants. For the first time in Edgar's life, money was rolling in.

Gertrude begged him to slow down. He could spare only the time for a brusque answer. "I've got to make up for all those long, lonely years you had to wait."

Blackburn begged him to take time for some readings. There were people who needed his healing powers. He said impatiently, "In a few days. Can't you see how everything is piling up on me right now? If I'm ever going to make it, I've got to make it now, when the business is booming."

They were prospering far above their fondest hopes.

One of the moments of triumph was when Edgar raced in to announce, "We landed the contract. We're to do all the photographs for the new spring catalog at the furniture factory."

He had figured out how to cut the last corner on costs. The factory would be closed on New Year's Day. He could go in early, wander at will, arrange his lights and reflectors and do all the photography without being annoyed by workmen and their dust and their schedules.

New Year's Day was cold, and all day the thermometer dropped. There was no heat at all in the factory. Shivering uncontrollably and blue with cold, Edgar kept on until the last photo was made. He returned to the studio in a daze of agony.

His two young assistants, Barnes and Porter, were there. They got him out of his coat and gloves and into a chair beside the glowing stove. He sat there for a few minutes, then quietly toppled forward on his face.

The boys lugged him to the couch and tried to revive him. When they discovered there was no sign of breathing, pulse, or heartbeat, they were terrified and bolted out to find doctors. Several came and worked futilely to resuscitate him.

They were discussing which undertaker to call when Blackburn walked in. He listened in stunned horror to what had occurred and what they had done. Edgar's lip was mashed and two teeth broken off where they had tried to force whisky down his throat. His feet were blistered raw from hot bricks. Each new arrival had tried a shot of morphine or strychnine without first checking with the others. Blackburn totaled these shots and blanched. Altogether, they had given Edgar enough of the deadly drugs to kill a horse.

Blackburn looked down at the body of his friend, the man who was like no other on earth. He tried every test without finding one sign of life, yet suddenly he knew with an unshakable conviction that Edgar Cayce was not dead.

"He's in a deep trance," he said, drawing a chair close. "I feel certain of it. If he is, maybe he'll respond to suggestion the way he does when he cures his own throat condition."

"You're wasting your time, John," one of the doctors said, buttoning his coat to leave. "You can't talk a corpse back to life."

The rest drifted out, leaving Blackburn alone, droning his suggestions over and over. "The body will return to normal condition. Breathing and heartbeat will resume, circulation will return to normal."

His voice grew hoarse with strain and sweat gathered on his forehead. Suddenly Edgar shuddered, sighed and opened his eyes. "Must sleep again," he mumbled. "Suggest the body heal itself."

Again breath and heartbeat ceased. Blackburn talked on and on. "The body will reject the poisons. It will heal the injuries."

After nearly an hour he saw that wherever a shot had been injected into Edgar's arm, the flesh was puffed out in a dark mound. Comprehension rushed over him. Obedient to his suggestion, Edgar's body had rejected the poisons and was holding them trapped just under the skin. He snatched an empty hypodermic and used it to suck out the fatal doses. Blood began to circulate again under the waxen skin.

Edgar opened his eyes. "I feel pretty good now, except where those butchers mangled me. Tell your brother, Dr. Jim, that he's finally going to get that dental work he's always teasing me about." Edgar slept around the clock and returned to the studio almost completely restored. However, he was more sober and thoughtful, and the frenzy of driving for business had subsided to a more reasonable activity.

"Don't ever scare me like that again," Blackburn told him. "You drove yourself until that guardian spirit or force of yours had to take you by the scruff of the neck and make you ease off. I'm convinced that's what happened to you."

"That was part of it," Edgar said soberly. "But I think it was a stiff warning, too. I was neglecting my readings. From now on I won't put any business ahead of that."

Despite his cutback in activity, the studio continued to prosper until there was more business than he and Frank Potter could handle. In the spring they opened a second studio over on College Street and Potter went to manage that. Edgar studied the growing bank account and began to look around for a fine house to buy.

He was baffled by one strange thing. When he tried to draw Gertrude into those grandiose dreams, she seemed only to half listen. Part of her consciousness seemed to have withdrawn into some remote, private world of her own. At times he would see her smiling to herself as if at some secret that was hers alone. Her eyes seemed particularly luminous. It was well into that winter before her swelling figure let him in on her secret.

Edgar stumbled around in a daze. "I'm going to be a father. Can you imagine that? I'm going to be a father."

Blackburn laughed. "It's been done before, old chap. You're really not so different, after all."

With all his varied interests, Edgar was never too busy to give readings, and the record of his successes mounted impressively. The committee of doctors was awed, and sometimes irritated.

"You certainly don't play favorites," one of them growled after a reading. "We consider ourselves the legitimate practitioners of medicine, but you're apt as not to tell us to go to hell and send patients to an osteopath or tell 'em all they need is a magnetic treatment or steam baths or massage."

"I guess I prescribe what the situation demands," Edgar said. "The cure is the thing, however it's accomplished."

"Damn it," another said, "it's frustrating to have you always turn out to be right. Take that woman who was supposed to have an immediate major operation. You told her to kick the doctors out, that all she had was a laceration of the stomach wall. You advised her to take a long hike and eat a raw lemon sprinkled with salt every day. It was so ridiculous that we kept a check on her so we could make a monkey out of you."

"Didn't it help her?" Edgar asked anxiously.

The doctor snorted. "In three weeks she was healthy as a horse. She walks ten miles a day now and could digest a cookstove. If you'd turn out to be wrong just once, we wouldn't feel so confoundedly useless with all our fancy degrees."

A Dr. Simmons, whose office was next door to the studio, became interested and asked Edgar to let him try an experimental reading. Edgar agreed and put himself to sleep on the doctor's couch.

During the reading, Father Harrigan, a local priest, dropped in to watch. He had just come from the post office and had an unopened package under his arm. "I just picked this up and I have no idea what's in it, Doctor. If your man's clairvoyant, as you say, let's see if he can tell us what's inside."

"Altar candles," Edgar said promptly. Edgar came out of his sleep and Father Harrigan looked at the doctor, crossed himself, and departed.

The Dean of Psychology at Potter College asked Edgar to give a demonstration before his class. During the reading, one of the girl students asked about the mysterious disappearance of funds that was draining away her father's business down in Mississippi. Edgar promptly described the thief and told exactly how the thefts were being accomplished.

A short time later he received a beautiful gold watch from the grateful psychology class, with a personal note that the girl's father had caught the thief and saved his business. Edgar worried a little about accepting the gift, but it was a very handsome watch; when there were no psychic repercussions he felt immensely relieved.

The doctors' committee was constantly being stunned by Edgar's uncanny power of clairvoyance. "The more we study you, the less we know," one of them said, "but it's obvious that something goes out from you during those trances and actually visits the person you're reading. The other day you described the room where a woman lay, down to the last detail of wall color, furnishings, and decorations. You even told who manufactured the bed and bedding. We checked and you had it absolutely right. Apparently your spirit or subconscious can go anywhere it wants to."

Edgar said wistfully, "I wish I didn't have to be asleep every time it happens. I've always had a yearning to visit strange places."

A local man dropped into the studio one evening when Edgar and the committee were sitting around. "I've got a friend in New York, a pretty successful real estate operator, who thinks he knows everything there is to know. I wrote him all about you a while back. His answer came today. He gives me the devil for being so gullible and says your stuff is all a fake."

"I'd like to make him eat those words," Edgar said angrily.

"Why not?" Blackburn suggested. "It'll be an interesting experiment, anyhow. Edgar, do you think you could find that man in New York and describe what he's doing at the time so completely that there can't be any question of your clairvoyance?"

"I don't know," Edgar said, "but I did that with some people in Paris once. I'm willing to try."

The reading was taken the next morning. "Yes, we have the body," Edgar said almost immediately after the suggestion. He gave the exact time. "He is coming along a busy street, stopping to speak to acquaintances on the way to his office. The street sign says it is William Street. He normally smokes cigarettes but this morning he feels like having a cigar. He stops in a cigar store and selects two."

Edgar went on, locating the cigar store, naming the brand. The man lit one, put the other in his pocket and went on to his office building. While the man waited for the elevator, Edgar said, "We'll have him walk upstairs so he'll remember it." He told of the man's growing impatient and finally taking the stairs, whistling "Annie Laurie."

A man was waiting in his office to discuss property at the end of the William Street bridge and a case concerning it that was coming up in surrogate court at three that afternoon. Afterward, the man sat down to open his mail. Edgar detailed a bill and a business letter. A third letter, from the man's sweetheart, he modestly refused to read, but he described a phone call from a man named Donagan.

The local man raced out to telegraph the full details to his friend in New York. Edgar glanced over the report on his reading. He said suddenly, "Hey, I made a mistake here. I said it was nine o'clock in the morning but it was only eight o'clock."

Blackburn grinned. "That's an extra convincer. You gave the correct New York time, which is one hour later than our Central Standard time."

"It is?" Edgar said blankly. "What do you know? I've learned something."

The local man came back, chuckling. "I'd give a million dollars to see that wise guy's face when he gets my wire."

An hour or so later they got an answering telegram. "Absolutely correct to last detail. Hang onto that man. Am taking next train for Bowling Green."

The New Yorker arrived, wild with enthusiasm to take Edgar to the metropolis. "You'll be a sensation. We'd clean up a fortune and you could cure a million people with your readings."

A local banker offered to lend Edgar any money he might need for the move. The doctors were frantic and Gertrude was in tears. "You mustn't even think of going, Edgar. That would really be abusing your power, no matter what that man promises you."

"All right," Edgar said, and added wistfully, "but I sure would like to see New York just once. It must be quite a sight."

The New Yorker hung around town for days, trying vainly to change Edgar's decision. At last he said, "All right. If you won't go, you won't go. But do me one favor. Give me a reading on some matters that are bothering me before I leave."

Edgar agreed. When he awoke, the man was gone, taking notes on the reading with him. Edgar went home to bed, feeling upset and irritable. His head ached abominably.

A week or so later the local man dropped in. "You sucker! I just got a letter from my friend in New York. He cleaned up twenty thousand dollars on information he got from your reading."

"That explains your headache that day," Gertrude said later when Edgar told her the news. "When your reading is used to help anyone in real need, you always awaken feeling refreshed. Whenever it is used for some material purpose, you feel terrible afterward. You'll have to be more careful about letting the wrong persons conduct readings."

By a slow process of trial and error, Edgar and his associates began to discover that not all readings on other than medical matters were necessarily harmful. Edgar's power was not averse to counseling in money matters if the purpose seemed legitimate.

A friend persuaded Edgar to try a reading in an effort to locate a buried treasure that was rumored to be somewhere close by. The answer came promptly. "Yes, we have the treasure. However, the land on which it lies does not belong to you. It belongs to someone else, and it would be right to give only him the location of the treasure." Since the power flatly refused to give even the general location, there was no way of discovering the rightful owner and helping him secure his prize.

Afterward Blackburn said thoughtfully, "Maybe I should ask about our old family treasure. It was buried by one of my ancestors during carpetbagger days and we still own the land, so there wouldn't be any question of ownership."

"Let's try it," Edgar suggested.

The reading was detailed but baffling. "Some of the landmarks are accurate and others I don't recognize," Blackburn said. "And you kept talking about the other house. That doesn't make sense because there's only one house there."

Eventually, in old family records, he learned that the original house had burned to the ground after the treasure was buried. The present house had been built a few feet off the first site so that part of it overlapped the old foundation. The Blackburn brothers puttered around and finally managed to locate some of the family silverware and jewelry where the reading said it would be. The main cache was somewhere under the newer house and never did come to light.

There was to be a meeting that fall with a large number of local and out-of-town doctors attending. Blackburn suggested, "Why not come along with me and give the crowd a demonstration. The more doctors you can get believing in you, the easier it will be to get them to follow your readings on patients."

Edgar agreed, with no premonition of what lay ahead. He lay down on a couch in front of the crowd and gave a demonstration reading on a patient under treatment by one of the physicians. He correctly diagnosed the case, described the patient and his surroundings, detailed the treatments being given, and ended by stating the precise temperature and pulse rate at the time.

A committee was hastily sent off to check the facts. In a short time they returned to verify everything Edgar had said, down to the finest detail.

Pandemonium broke out in the hall. Doctors who had never seen Edgar before crowded up for a closer look, arguing noisily over whether he was in a trance, a hypnotic state, or some kind of strange seizure. They elbowed the protesting Blackburn aside and began to pinch and poke at Edgar, lifting his eyelids to peer into his eyes and prying open his mouth.

"He can't feel a thing," one said. "Completely anaesthetized, and I'll prove it."

Before Blackburn could elbow his way back, his angry protests unheeded, they had jabbed Edgar with pins, rammed a hatpin completely through his cheek and pried under one fingernail with a knife blade. There was neither nervous reaction nor blood.

In a fury, Blackburn forced his colleagues back and gave the command to awaken. Edgar sat up and cried out in pain. Blood began to pour out of his wounds.

"It's nothing serious, my boy," one of the doctors said pompously. "We were merely making a few simple tests."

Edgar sprang up. "Tests!" he shouted. "That's all any of you can think of. I thought I had friends who cared enough to see me treated like a human being. But I'm not a human being to anybody, and I have no friends."

Blackburn laid a soothing hand on his arm, but he flung it off. "Get away from me. None of you will ever lay a hand on me again. You thought I was a fake, but you're the fakes. You won't even talk plain English for fear your patient will understand how little any of you know about a human body. Well, I'm through with the lot of you and this whole business forever. I'll never submit to another test or experiment or give a reading for anybody but a person in real need. The whole pack of you can go straight to hell!" He left the building angrily.

Chapter Twelve

IN A FEW DAYS Edgar learned of Blackburn's unsuccessful attempts to protect him, and their friendship was resumed. Blackburn was caring for Gertrude during her pregnancy and continued to serve as conductor when Edgar gave readings. People had been spreading their stories of being healed by Edgar's power, and requests were coming in from all over the country. Edgar never turned down any that seemed genuinely urgent, but he refused to have anything more to do with the doctors' committee. The wound under his fingernail became infected and bothered him all winter.

He began to drive himself harder at the studio. The imminent family increase, with its attendant increase in expenses, set him to worrying about money again. It was still not piling up fast enough to suit him and his needs.

To boost Christmas business, he took a $40,000 consignment of prints, paintings, and water colors from a New York dealer and opened an exhibition in the College Street studio. The paintings were too expensive for the local market, but the other items sold like wildfire. Edgar shipped the paintings back to New York and arranged to hold the remainder of his consignment through Christmas.

He felt such a surge of optimism that he stopped looking at houses to buy and began to study architects' plans and building costs.

The night before Christmas Eve of 1906 he was awakened by excited shouts and a loud hammering on the door.

Edgar called out sleepily. A frantic voice yelled,

"You better get downtown as fast as you can. Your studio on College Street is on fire."

By the time he got there, the building was a smoking ruin. Somewhere in that charred shell was nearly $10,000 worth of pictures. His insurance covered only permanent stock and fixtures, not merchandise on consignment.

"We're wiped out," he groaned to Gertrude, "completely ruined. We haven't a thing left."

"We have each other," she soothed him. "And soon we'll have our baby."

Every penny of savings went toward reducing the debt, but the unpaid remainder loomed like a mountain to Edgar. He plunged into operations at the State Street studio with new fury, working night and day against the protests of both Gertrude and Blackburn.

Edgar's partner, Potter, decided to get out and sold his interest to Gertrude's brother, Lynn, and a man named Adcock. Business was good, but all profit went to pay off debts. Edgar grew haggard and irritable again, but no one could make him slow down.

His son was born on the afternoon of March 16, 1907, two days before Edgar's thirtieth birthday. He was a healthy, husky baby, and they named him Hugh Lynn Cayce, after Gertrude's two brothers. Edgar plunged back into his work more fiercely than ever.

"You're asking for it," Blackburn warned him glumly. . . .

A few days later he brought Edgar a plea for a reading for a Mrs. Garvey, a local woman whose illness defied the doctors and who was growing rapidly worse. Edgar sighed wearily. "I'll do it, but I can't spare the time now. Arrange it for eight tonight. I'll finish up here and meet you at my place."

He got home a few minutes early and refused his supper until after the reading. He played with Hugh Lynn a few moments, then felt so exhausted that he threw himself down across the bed to rest until Blackburn arrived.

When he opened his eyes it was dark. His watch read four minutes past two. He jumped up in a panic and stumbled out into the lighted parlor. Gertrude sat on the

98

couch, weeping, and Blackburn was pacing back and forth, grim and white-faced. Gertrude threw herself into his arms. "I've been almost out of my mind. I couldn't waken you and neither could Dr. Blackburn. You weren't even breathing and I thought you were dead. Dr. Blackburn said you were just getting what you had coming to you."

"I warned you," Blackburn growled. "I knew it was another deep trance like the last time, but it still scared the blazes out of me. I wish you'd quit driving yourself too hard."

"Oh, Lord," Edgar cried in sudden alarm. "I promised that reading at eight o'clock, and I've let that poor woman down. If she's worse now, I'll never forgive myself. I've got to get over there right away. Maybe it still isn't too late."

He and Blackburn hurried through the silent streets, the sound of their feet echoing in the still night air. The Garvey house was ablaze with lights. Edgar groaned aloud and ran up onto the porch.

Garvey came to the door and Edgar blurted, "Your wife—is she—"

Garvey seized his hand, crying, "Bless you, my boy. Oh, heaven bless you."

From upstairs a woman's voice called strongly, "Is that you, Edgar Cayce? I don't know how you did it, but I woke up at four minutes past two, feeling like a million dollars and hungry as a bear. Will you tell that fool husband of mine to let me get out of this bed and fix myself a square meal?"

On the way home, Edgar said soberly, "I've learned one thing that makes me feel better. As long as I'm honestly trying to do right and help people in need, my power or whatever it is sees to it that I don't betray their faith."

"I know something that would make me feel better," Blackburn snapped. "That would be your promise to quit trying to become the most solvent man in the cemetery."

Gertrude's Aunt Lizzie had come to help out with the

baby. Edgar had managed to find a small, ramshackle cottage that was more suitable for a family than the furnished rooms, though not much more spacious. He never approached the place without a feeling of bitterness over the fine home and good living that should have been theirs. The need for money was a constant spur that roweled him night and day.

About that time Edgar began to realize that there had been so many important advances in photography that he was becoming hopelessly outdated. His old-fashioned methods and equipment were eating into profits and more up-to-date rivals were steadily luring away business. Edgar tried to catch up by studying books and trade journals, but he found the task almost hopeless. His lack of education made the technical descriptions impossible to understand.

He finally yielded to necessity and arranged to take a short summer course at a photographic school in McMinville, Tennessee. Lizzie agreed to stay with Gertrude and the baby. Lynn and Adcock would run the studio.

He was preparing to leave when his father came over from Hopkinsville. "Son, you've used this great gift of yours generously to help other people. I hate to do this, but I've come to ask you to use it in helping your own family. Business has been bad for a long time. The girls are helping out, but it's pretty hard keeping things going."

"I'll do all I can, Dad," Edgar said. "You know how I've had to operate since the fire, but—"

The squire lifted his hand. "I don't want money, son. Not from you. I want some readings. The wheat market is booming right now, but it's up and down. A group of fellows back home have formed a combine and pooled a good sum of cash to put into the market. They've offered me a full share in exchange for a few readings that'll tell them exactly what to do. That share could mean an awful lot to your mother and me right now."

Edgar was stunned. His whole being rebelled against the idea. He tried to protest, but the squire was insistent, and finally Edgar agreed, stipulating that he himself was to get no benefit in any form.

When he awoke from the first reading his head ached. The squire was on the telephone, gleefully repeating instructions to his associates in Hopkinsville. Edgar stumbled home to Gertrude, who tried to comfort him and hide her own worry over the possible outcome.

With Edgar's readings, the syndicate prospered from the start. The squire reported pyramiding profits in awe. When Edgar wanted to stop, the squire was horrified and pleaded for just a few more sessions of advice.

One day the reading said, "A man named Leiter will corner the wheat market. Wheat will reach a dollar nineteen, then plunge abruptly to the bottom."

This was so fantastic that the syndicate talked it over and decided for once Edgar's power was running wild. Even the squire was dubious. In the end they voted to ignore that reading and continue along the line they had been following so profitably. The next day Edgar's prediction came true and all their profits were wiped out.

There was resentment and bitterness. The group of men blamed Edgar and his father for somehow cheating them.

For days after the crash, Edgar suffered violent headaches and nausea. He tried to give readings for people in genuine need and found his power had vanished. Most of the time he was unable to put himself to sleep. Once or twice he went into a deep sleep and lay for hours, refusing to speak. The only suggestion that brought response was the one to awaken.

"I've done it this time," he told Gertrude miserably. "I wouldn't heed the warnings. I abused my power and now it's been taken away. But at least I haven't lost my power to work. I'll hurry through the photographic course and when I get back home we'll make the studio really boom."

On the train to McMinville he began to feel more cheerful. His headaches had gone and his spirits were rising at the interesting prospect of living in new surroundings.

He was quite cheerful when he enrolled in the new school and he found the studies not nearly as hard as he had feared. He wrote gay letters home and revived his old dreams of ease and affluence.

The president of the school was interested in hypnotism, and had heard reports of Edgar's powers. He wanted to get together for long discussions and was shocked when Edgar told him flatly, "I've lost that power, and good riddance. Now I don't want to talk or even think about it anymore. I just want to learn to be a better photographer."

On the way to his room that evening he started to answer a greeting from a fellow student. Nothing came out but a rasping whisper.

Chapter Thirteen

EDGAR STOOD in the shadowy twilight, sweating and shaking. Over and over he tried to force out a normal voice. The effort tore at his throat and produced nothing but a whisper.

For a little time he had wallowed in his new sense of freedom; now that brief delusion was gone. Whatever its purpose, a stern and inflexible psychic puppeteer still held the strings that controlled his life.

Another realization came to haunt him. Since his misuse of the power, he had lost the ability to hypnotize himself at will. Unless that ability returned, there was no way to restore his voice. Worse, there was no one closer than Bowling Green who knew how to help him treat himself. Or was there someone?

The president of the photographic school had been just about to sit down to his supper when the doorbell rang. He answered and bent close to make out Edgar's hoarse whisper.

"I've heard about that trick voice of yours," he said. "Come on into the library. There's a couch there. You write out what I'm supposed to say and I'll do my best to help you. The supper can wait, but a chance like this can't!"

Edgar lay back on the rich leather of the couch and closed his eyes. *Sleep! Go into a deep, deep sleep! Oh please, dear Lord, let me sleep again!* A swirling darkness enfolded him.

He opened his eyes and tried a tentative, fearful "hello." It came out clear and strong. He sat up, beaming. "It worked. My voice is back. I can't thank you enough."

They sat talking until past midnight. When they parted at last, Edgar had agreed to try a reading again if someone could be found with a genuine need. When a suitable subject was finally located, a new hitch developed. Edgar refused to give a reading unless at least one reputable physician were on hand to interpret and apply the information safely—and no local doctor would listen to such a preposterous idea.

Eventually Edgar finished his course and went home without having given any reading for his benefactor, but he left a deep impression that would eventually lead to a curious result.

Edgar got home to a warm welcome. It became altogether too warm a few nights later when the State Street studio was gutted by fire. This time, however, his insurance coverage was complete and the adjusters sympathetic. Within three weeks they were open again, with more modern equipment.

A few mornings later Edgar came down to find Adcock ahead of him. His partner had the firm's books spread out on a desk and the floor was littered with pages of figures. He turned a harried face to Edgar and blurted, "My God, we're in terrible shape. I've just been adding up all our debts and it's awful."

"We owe a lot," Edgar admitted, "but business is good and we're paying it off steadily."

"A penny at a time, and only as long as the creditors feel like letting us. Any one of them can demand his full due at any time, and throw us into bankruptcy because we can't pay up."

"But they're not doing it," Edgar pointed out. "Every creditor knows we had bad luck and they're being more than patient with us. Nobody is pressing us for payment."

"That doesn't mean they won't," Adcock said, mopping his forehead. "You're talking about buying a lot of new lights and cameras and darkroom equipment to run us deeper into debt. I can't take any more."

"What are you going to do?" Edgar asked.

"Get out while I still can," Adcock said grimly. "I'm putting the studio into voluntary bankruptcy today."

Edgar leaned against the wall, sick from this new blow. "If that's what you mean to do, I guess I can't stop you."

"You damn well better not try," Adcock said and went out the door.

His petition was granted, and a creditors' committee appointed to work out a settlement. Everyone was sympathetic and regretful over the move. "This is only a formality," Edgar told them grimly. "Bankruptcy or not, every one of you will get his money in full. I promise you that."

In the midst of the meeting, Gertrude's Aunt Carrie arrived. Gertrude had telephoned her about the bankruptcy and she had taken the next train, bringing along her new husband, Dr. Thomas House.

"As the principal creditor," Carrie told the group, "I've got the say about what happens. I'll say it. The studio stays open, with Edgar running it and paying his debts, the way he always has. Any objections?" There were none.

Edgar plunged back into the business, but the old zest and burning ambition was gone. His hard luck had made him sick of the studio, the town, of everything he had once found so enchanting.

Gertrude shared his disillusionment, but not his bitterness. "This can't go on forever, Edgar. We'll get ahead some day," she said.

"When we're old and broken," Edgar said. "The only goal I can work for now is to pay off our debts, and when I finally reach that we'll be right where we started—dead broke."

Carrie decided to stay on for a time and let Lizzie return to Hopkinsville. Dr. House planned to start practicing in Hopkinsville in the spring, but meanwhile he wanted a chance to loaf. He was a bluff, friendly, capable man. To give more thorough help to his patients he had studied and qualified as both an M.D. and an osteopath.

Edgar had liked Tom House from the start. "With

105

that background, you ought to be checking my readings. They're as liable to prescribe osteopathy as medicine."

House snorted genially. "Don't talk to me about that business. Everybody in the family's been trying to fill me up with it. I refuse to listen to anything that goes contrary to common sense and my years of schooling. Don't forget, I've got degrees in two fields, not just one. That means I've had twice as much grounding in skepticism, Edgar. So let's not drag ourselves into silly arguments."

Edgar shrugged and dropped the subject. Dr. Blackburn, who dropped in every day, met the same rebuff when he tried to tell House about some of the cases. Whenever he and Edgar fell to discussing a reading, House would puff his pipe and withdraw into thoughts until the talk finally swung back to comprehensible things.

Edgar had begun to give readings again for Blackburn. He was relieved to find that his power had returned undiminished. In the late fall he received a letter from the president of the photo school in McMinville. The president's brother was a division superintendent for the Southern Railway. There had been a bad wreck on the line and the brother was deeply concerned over the cause. He wondered if one of Edgar's readings might reveal the information. Edgar, grateful for the president's help in restoring his voice, was happy to try.

The reading laid the blame for the accident squarely on one man, giving details of the negligence that was responsible. He sent the information along and presently got a report on it.

"My brother was impressed with the reading, but his superiors refused to pay any attention. The man you blamed is an old and trusted employee and they refuse even to confront him with your findings, which they consider ridiculous."

A short time after this Edgar got a letter from a vice president of the railroad. "No one would act on your information about the wreck, but I find I can't get the matter off my mind. Would it be possible to obtain another of your readings in hope of getting further details?

If what you said is true, we still have a potential cause of further accidents in our organization."

The second reading was curt and blunt. "If he who has been named as the cause is allowed to remain in the service, he will, before the first of December, be the direct cause of an accident that will be the death of the one who refused the information. This will happen in Virginia and West Virginia."

Blackburn read over the warning and shook his head. "That's certainly straight from the shoulder. But I don't get one part. How can one accident happen in two states? It sounds a little crazy to me."

Edgar shrugged and sent it along, but the vice president never acknowledged it. From the photo school president, Edgar learned that the railroad officials had considered the warning as the raving of a lunatic, and had tossed it into the wastebasket.

On November 29th, the switchman who had been accused in the first reading was working at a division point on the Virginia-West Virginia line. When he left for the night he forgot to throw a siding switch. The vice president who had written to Edgar was asleep in his private car on that siding. Around midnight the fast express came through and was hurled onto the siding because of the neglected switch. The impact shattered the private car and drove it across the state line. The vice president died while they were still trying to get him out of the wreckage.

Edgar and Blackburn were both shaken by the accuracy of the prophecy. Blackburn ran his nervous hands through his hair. "This is out of my class, Edgar. I've had a tough enough time accepting your psychic diagnoses, but at least they deal with a field I know something about. This is a brand-new aspect of that fantastic power of yours, whatever it is. I don't understand it and I don't like it. I don't think I even want to have anything to do with any more readings that aren't medical."

"I know how you feel," Edgar said. "It scares me, too."

Blackburn was due to receive a worse fright before the week was out. Layne's stories and Edgar's subsequent demonstrations had made a deep impression on everyone at the Southern School of Osteopathy. A few days after the train wreck incident, Edgar received a letter from the founder of the school, asking for a physical reading on an infantile paralysis victim.

As the reading progressed, Edgar began to talk too fast for Blackburn's racing pencil. Still writing furiously, Blackburn put his left hand out toward Edgar and muttered absently, "Hold up, there. Not so fast."

At the word "up" Edgar's reclining figure floated up from the couch and hovered, without support, against Blackburn's extended hand. He yelped and snatched his hand away. Edgar's body fell back to the couch and after a moment the reading continued.

When Edgar awakened, Blackburn was pacing the floor nervously. "I don't know what's happening to you, but I wish it would quit. A lot of doctors say I'm crazy for conducting these readings, and if you keep on jolting my nerves with tricks like that, I'll be ready to believe them."

"I don't do it on purpose," Edgar said. "I don't even know that I do it, but I wish I'd stop, too."

He began to worry again and get back his old terrors about the source of his uncanny power.

With spring, Carrie and Dr. House went back to Hopkinsville, taking Gertrude and Hugh Lynn along for a visit at home. Edgar moved into the studio and worked harder than ever. He was afraid to continue the readings, but more afraid of the penalties if he stopped. As a compromise, he tried to confine them to only the most desperate cases. The only comfort for him was that so far there had been not one failure in the mounting score of readings.

One night he got a phone call from Dr. House. "Can you get over here right away? Carrie's desperately sick. The doctors want to operate immediately, but she won't let them touch her until she's had one of your readings. If we don't humor her, she may delay until it's too late."

"I'll be there on the next train," Edgar promised.

He sat through the long ride, tormented by fears. For

a little while he had begun to believe implicitly in the rightness of his power. Now, when doubts had come back to haunt him, he faced the terrible test on someone close to him. He prayed desperately, but he could not expel the demons of fear.

Carrie herself had no doubts. From her sick bed she said weakly, "Your diagnoses have never been wrong yet and they won't be wrong now. Tell me what to do."

There was no one but Dr. House to conduct the reading. He listened in grim silence while Edgar gave him the instructions. Then he said through clenched teeth: "I'm doing this only to humor Carrie. If we understand each other, let's hurry and get this over with."

When Edgar awoke Dr. House was talking soberly with the specialist. Carrie gave him a wan smile. "They say I have a tumor. You say I have a stoppage of the bowel. I'm still on your side, Edgar." She added, smiling, "You also said I was pregnant."

Dr. House turned from his low-voiced conference, his jaw set. "We've decided the treatment you prescribed can't do any serious harm. We still have time to give it a try. Then I want it clearly understood that we'll stop this nonsense and get on with the operation."

Edgar went slowly downstairs, his mind in a turmoil. If only he could find the simple implicit faith that Carrie had. There was only one consolation. The doctors agreed that his treatment would not make the situation worse. He slumped into a chair and fell into an exhausted sleep.

He awoke with Dr. House pumping his hand fervently. "Don't ask me to believe what I can't, but you were right. We tried your treatment and Carrie is like a new woman. The trouble was exactly what you said." Then he sobered. "I mean to say, you were half right. I'd give anything in the world if you could have hit it a hundred per cent this morning."

"What do you mean?" Edgar asked blankly.

"You said Carrie was pregnant. That part is impossible. She has been examined by the best doctors. There's no question at all about their findings. My wife can never have a baby."

Edgar was overjoyed at having correctly diagnosed Carrie's illness, but the mistake about her pregnancy worried him. "I can't understand it. As far as I know a reading has never been wrong before."

"Don't worry about it," Dr. House said jovially. "There's no harm done, you were right about the important part. Nobody's infallible."

"The psychic diagnoses always were right before," Edgar repeated worriedly.

The small error stuck in his mind and festered there, pouring a subtle doubt into his own self-confidence. If he could make one mistake, he could make others, and the next one might be far more serious.

He worried about it right up to the day that Carrie Salter House gave premature birth to the baby the specialists all knew she could never have.

Meanwhile Edgar stayed in Hopkinsville for a few days of relaxation with Gertrude and Hugh Lynn and some visits with his own family. Old friends and neighbors came around to see him. One of these was a professor in the high school, a man who had been born and raised in Canada. In the course of an evening's visit he told of a murder that had taken place recently back in his home town.

"I knew the murdered woman well," he told them. "She and her sister were old maids, queer ducks and practically misers, who lived in the old family home with stores of money hidden around, according to the rumor. I guess some prowler believed it, because he broke into the house one night. One of the women heard him, got out of bed, and came to the head of the stairs. When she called to ask who was there, he shot her and got clean away. The other sister ran out and saw her body tumbling to the foot of the stairs. They've grilled every suspect and vagrant around the countryside, without turning up a single clue. I hate to think a murderer as callous as that is roaming free among my friends there, maybe waiting to kill again."

"I'll bet Edgar could put himself to sleep and tell who

110

did it. That boy can do anything in his sleep," the squire said.

The idea appealed to them and they persuaded Edgar to try a reading. A moment after he fell asleep he was giving all the details of the crime. There had been no prowler, he stated; one sister had killed the other because of rivalry over a suitor. "She shot her sister at the head of the stairs and watched the body tumble to the foot, where it was found by the police. She then threw the murder pistol out of an upstairs window. It landed in the eave trough and was carried down the drain spout by a heavy downpour of rain. It is lying now in the mud beneath the bottom of the spout." He went on to give the number on the pistol and tell exactly how its ownership could be traced and proven.

The friend was so impressed that on the way home that night he telegraphed the full details to the Canadian police. The following afternoon the local sheriff drove up to the Cayce house, where Edgar and his father were talking on the porch.

"I'm surprised to see you here, Eddie," he said to Edgar. "A wanted criminal like you, I sure figured you'd be high-tailin' it for the tall timber by now."

"What the blazes are you talking about?" the squire demanded.

The sheriff chuckled. "It seems Eddie went into one of his trances and told all about some murder up in Canada. The police found the gun right where he said it would be and got a confession out of the killer. They phoned me to nab Edgar quick. They said nobody but an accomplice who was on the scene during the crime could know all the little details, including the number on the gun. However, I reckon I can smooth it out for you somehow."

A day or two before Edgar returned to Bowling Green, an old friend of the squire's dropped in on his way through town. He was a private detective, currently hunting for a fortune in stolen bonds for which a large reward had been offered. The squire immediately proposed a reading. Again Edgar agreed, with reluctance.

The reading described the man who had stolen the bonds, but said he was helped by a woman on the inside. They were currently staying together in a hotel in western Pennsylvania and had the bonds with them. The woman was described as having a small red birthmark on her thigh and two toes on her left foot grown together as the result of a childhood burn.

When Edgar awoke, the detective was on the long-distance telephone, excitedly repeating the information to the owner of the bonds. From the couch he could hear the furious bellow that erupted from the receiver.

"I don't recognize the man who stole my bonds, but the woman with him couldn't be anybody but my wife. She told me she was going to Chicago to visit her sister."

The nervous fugitives had fled only an hour before police closed in on the Pennsylvania hotel Edgar had named. Now Edgar was committed, and he had to stay over for five unhappy days while subsequent readings followed the couple to Columbus, Ohio, to be captured at last in a hotel he had identified.

"I'm not going to do that again," he told Gertrude miserably. "Even if they were crooks and deserved to be caught, I don't like feeling that my power is being used to hound and punish anyone."

"I'm glad," Gertrude said. "I didn't like it, either. You were given your gift to use in healing the sick. Whenever you use it for any other purpose, I'm frightened and unhappy, and I know you are, too."

Chapter Fourteen

BACK IN BOWLING GREEN once more, Edgar plunged into his interrupted bill-paying drive. One by one the studio creditors were being paid off for their faith and patience, but that satisfaction was tempered by one nagging question: When will I be able to repay Gertrude for her faith and patience?

She was a wonderful budgeteer. Thanks to her they were managing to live comfortably on the barest minimum, while the lion's share of income went to creditors. Edgar never ceased to marvel at her efficiency, her practicality, and her unfaltering trust in him. It hurt him every time he saw her making do with her old household equipment.

One of their happiest moments came when Edgar was summoned back to Hopkinsville to give a reading on Carrie's baby. The child had been frail and sickly from its birth, and now convulsions had begun to sap what strength the tiny body held. Edgar would never forget the wracking torment of that night.

His reading prescribed a deadly overdose of belladonna, to be followed by a powerful antidote. The doctors raged and Edgar himself was sick with fear. Again it was Carrie's unshakable faith that decided the issue. She herself administered the poison and the antidote—and she was not even surprised when the convulsions ceased and little Tom, Jr., began to cry healthily.

Edgar's joy overflowed when Dr. House said, "I never believed in your stuff; I wouldn't let myself. Carrie had the faith that could never be shaken. From now on, Edgar, there will be two of us here with that faith. I can't understand, but I believe."

On such firm foundations he longed to build his own faith. He would believe in himself for a little while and then inevitably some tiny seed of doubt would be sown to make him question the source of his power. If it were truly a gift from God, why was he ever permitted to misuse it? The power, as manifested through the readings, had never yet made a mistake, but it permitted Edgar to make them over and over. It was this discrepancy that kept him frightened and unsure.

His most terrible experience came soon after he returned, full of new confidence, from saving Carrie's baby. One evening a young man he knew well came to the studio. He was younger than Edgar, a junior bank clerk struggling to support a wife and baby and prepare for a second child on an inadequate salary. He was always worried, but this night he was on the verge of panic.

"You've got to help me, Edgar. I've got to get hold of a lot of money fast, and you've got the only system I know. You can go into one of those trances of yours and tell me the winners at Latonia race track tomorrow."

"Absolutely not," Edgar said flatly. "My power can't be used for purposes like that. I made that mistake once and the consequences were terrible; I'll never make it again. I'm sorry. Good night."

Edgar turned toward the darkroom. The clerk caught his sleeve with a shaking hand. "You better listen, before you walk out on me. You wouldn't sleep too well if you knew you had one or two deaths on your conscience. I'm not asking this for myself."

Edgar stopped, looking at the pale, twisted face. "What are you trying to say? What's wrong?"

"I've been betting at Latonia, trying to get one winner to pull us out of the hole and get my wife the care she needs. I thought I had a sure thing, but I lost. I heard afterward that the race was fixed. That crooked race cleaned me out. It wasn't my money, Edgar."

"The bank's?"

"I was so sure I could put it right back. They're auditing the books Monday and they'll spot it right away.

I'll go to prison. The shame will kill my wife and the baby she's carrying. In three races tomorrow I could win enough to put all the money back in time. Then I'd never gamble again. I swear it."

"No," Edgar answered hoarsely. "I can't, and I won't. You mustn't ask me again. I'm sorry for you, but you'll have to find some other solution." He shook off his friend's detaining hand and plunged into the darkroom.

The young man's voice came through the door. "Think about it some more tonight, Edgar. Think of the price the innocent will pay. I'll stop in tomorrow morning on my way to work."

Edgar spent the night pacing the floor in an agony of indecision. No scruple, no promise, no fear of reprisal could stand large in his mind against his friend's warning that the innocent would suffer the consequences. By morning he made up his mind: he would give the reading.

He fully expected to feel terrible after the reading and he braced himself to bear the penalties with stoicism. To his surprise, the reaction this time was comparatively mild. The inevitable headache was a dull weight on his brain rather than the violent skull-crackers of other times. He felt depleted and tired, as usual after a reading of dubious purpose.

The only difference was that this time the condition persisted instead of clearing up. Each day the headache throbbed, and Edgar grew more and more listless. He felt drained of vital force. Blackburn grew alarmed and insisted Edgar take a reading on himself. The moment he lay down on the couch, Edgar understood what it was that had left him. He had no power left to hypnotize himself. They tried desperately, day after day, with no result. The force that had spoken through Edgar Cayce was gone.

It was more than two weeks afterward that one of the doctors who still dropped in at the studio frequently remarked one night, "That was a sad business about that young friend of yours."

Edgar looked up quickly. "What about him?"

"I thought you'd heard. He made a big killing at the

races a while back, and I guess he couldn't stand prosperity. He quit his job at the bank and went on a drunken spree that lasted so long his wife left him and went back to her folks. The bank finally turned up a big shortage in his accounts and went looking for him. They caught up with him last night, but he won't have to go to jail. The excessive drinking had done something to his brain. He was hauled off to the insane asylum this morning, raving mad."

Edgar stumbled into the darkroom, bleak with horror. He looked up into the darkness, whispering, "Why? Why did you let me do it? Why didn't you take my power away before I destroyed him? I can't know what's right every time. Why didn't you stop me?"

Edgar went downhill rapidly. Tortured by remorse, he spent most of his nights pacing the floor. When sheer exhaustion brought him snatches of sleep, he was haunted by nightmares. His weight dropped, and with it his vitality. Pleas for readings were still coming in and he was still forcing himself to try, but not even the most urgent need brought any response. The force had gone out of him.

"Look here," Blackburn told him frantically. "This can't go on, Edgar. You're a sick man. I've hated to tell you this, but you've got tuberculosis. If you don't get out of here and rest, you'll be dead before Christmas."

Edgar went off without answering. He had films to develop and a sitting to arrange. Somewhere he was dredging up the strength to go on with his work. Solvency danced ahead of him like a will-o'-the-wisp.

Gertrude had stayed on in Hopkinsville to save house rent, so she was spared the knowledge of what was happening to Edgar. She knew only that his letters were arriving less and less frequently, oddly short and strained. Intuitively she knew something was wrong and wrote, begging him to come home for a rest.

On a blazing hot day in August, 1909, he scrawled a check, attached it to a bill and sat staring at it while comprehension slowly seeped into his mind. This was the last bill, the last penny of debt paid off. He was free at last from the burden that had weighed him down for

116

so many years. He tried to feel a sense of exultation, of triumph, but he felt only tired.

He looked at the check stubs. There was just about enough money left in the account for a ticket to Hopkinsville. He wrote his last check to himself and went to pack his suitcase.

Blackburn found him just locking the studio door. "Thank God you've at last got sense enough to take care of yourself. Don't come back until you're completely well."

"I'll never be back," Edgar said. "Too much has happened in Bowling Green for me to ever live here again. I'm through."

"What about the studio?"

"I'm selling the equipment for anything I can get. It will keep us until I can get on my feet again and get a job."

"Well, damn it," Blackburn said fiercely, "let me carry that suitcase to the train for you. You don't look as if you have the strength left to carry a handkerchief."

Everyone in Hopkinsville was shocked at his appearance. Gertrude hid her own horror and fussed over him until he broke down and told her of his friend and the reason behind his own decline. She clung to him fiercely, comforting him, giving him some of her strength until he could find his own.

She had unpacked his suitcase and laid his old, worn Bible on the stand beside the bed. He picked it up one day and sat down to read; it had been so long since he had taken time for the stories that had once thrilled him so deeply. Now he felt a stirring of the old feeling, and a sense of peace.

He read on and on. Gertrude came to the door, saw him completely absorbed in his Bible, and tiptoed quietly away. For the first time since Edgar arrived, a smile lifted the shadow of fear from her face.

The moment marked the beginning of Edgar's return to health. "I think I'm beginning to understand," he told Gertrude one night. "God's will is never forced on man. The promise is there, and the way, but man must make

117

the choice and reach his own hand out for the gift. I had a power and misused it, so that power was taken away. I don't know whether or not I'll ever get it back, but if I do I know I'll never abuse it again. I used to ask for signs to guide me and when I got no answer, I began to doubt. The answer was right here in the Bible all the time. When I'm not sure of the path again, I'll know where to look for the guide marks."

"Then you'll get your power back," Gertrude said with quiet assurance. "It may not be soon, but it will come."

"I hope so," Edgar said. "There are so many to be helped, so many I could be helping right now if only I hadn't lost faith."

He came back from the post office one day, walking with a new assurance. "I've got a job. A man from the photo school has a studio down in Anniston, Alabama. He's offered me the same kind of partnership deal I used to have with Bowles. I'm to go around taking pictures in Calhoun and Talladega Counties. As soon as I've made enough money, I'll send for you and Hugh Lynn."

"We'll be lonely," she said, "but it won't be so bad, now that you're well and there's something to look forward to. Before we know it, we'll have our own studio again in some nice town, and bad times will be behind us."

In the new job with Russell Brothers, Edgar had long, lonely trips between towns. Often he packed only necessary equipment on his back and set out on foot through the woods. The solitude for meditation and the renewed communion with nature completed the healing of his body and mind and soul.

He wrote Gertrude jubilantly, "I'm positive my power has come back. There has been no chance to try a reading and nobody here to conduct one, but I have a very definite feeling that when the time comes that someone needs help, I'll be able to give it. You have no idea how wonderful it is to feel whole again."

Almost immediately he got a letter from the head of the State Normal School at Jacksonville, Alabama, a man who had heard of Edgar's power through friends and had corresponded with him earlier. Now he begged Edgar to try a reading for a student who was very ill. Edgar went there at once.

With the school president as conductor and two local physicians as witnesses, he gave three readings with remarkable success. His letters to Gertrude fairly bubbled with joy.

When he went home for the holidays, his father told him of a new doctor in town who was very anxious to meet Edgar. He was a homeopath named Wesley Ketchum, a breezy and personable young man.

"I've heard a lot about you and your readings," he told Edgar when they shook hands. "In fact, you turned my landlady's hair white overnight."

"I did?" Edgar said blankly.

Ketchum laughed. "She used to be a very sick red-head until one of your readings told her she was being poisoned by her hair dye. She quit using it and now she's a very healthy white-head."

He was eager to witness a reading, but Edgar shook his head. "I don't give them anymore, except on a written request from a person in real need."

Ketchum dashed out and returned shortly with a written plea for a psychic diagnosis. The squire conducted the reading. At its conclusion Ketchum was gleeful. The reading had been on himself and concerned a persistent pain in his side that had been repeatedly diagnosed as appendicitis. Ketchum had already made arrangements for an operation. The reading said there was no appendicitis, that the pain came from a spinal lesion resulting from a fall long before.

"You sure sounded convincing." Ketchum grinned. "If I'd heard that diagnosis given for someone else, I'd probably have swallowed it. It was your hard luck that you tried it on one fellow in a position to know the real facts of the case and able to expose your trick."

Edgar left the house in a rage. Ketchum hunted up an osteopath to confirm his opinion that Edgar was a

119

bare-faced fraud. Without seeing the reading, the osteopath verified every word of Edgar's diagnosis. He made the simple adjustment described in the reading and Ketchum's pain vanished. He went out to find Edgar and offer his abject apologies. . . .

In the early spring Ketchum phoned Edgar in Alabama and offered him his fare home and back to conduct a reading for a desperately ill patient. Edgar accepted, partly because it meant a chance to see Gertrude and his young son for a couple of days.

Following his usual custom, Edgar gave the reading without learning the identity of the patient. He heard no more about the case or the result of his reading for several months. Meanwhile he had taken a job with better pay at a photo studio in Montgomery, Alabama.

He awoke one morning to find the whole story headlined across the newspapers of the nation. Overnight an obscure photographer had become an international sensation. The name of Edgar Cayce was on every tongue, the story of his remarkable power the subject of every conversation.

He was stunned, outraged—and famous.

not the slightest knowledge of medicine when not in that condition. . . .

The rest of the story covered Ketchum's medical paper and elaborated on specific cases and Edgar's personal history. It also added information that would come as a not altogether pleasant surprise to Edgar. Ketchum had never bothered to tell him that during one of the readings, he had slipped in the suggestion that Edgar's power explain itself.

When asked to give the source of his knowledge, he being then in the subconscious state, he stated: "Edgar Cayce's mind is amenable to suggestion, the same as all other subconscious minds, but in addition, it has the power to interpret to the objective mind of others what it acquires from the subconscious mind of other individuals of the same kind. The subconscious mind forgets nothing. The conscious mind receives the impression from without and transfers all thought to the subconscious, where it remains even though the conscious be destroyed." He described himself as a third person, saying further that his subconscious mind is in direct communication with all other subconscious minds, and is capable of interpreting through his objective mind and imparting impressions received to other objective minds, gathering in this way all the knowledge possessed by millions of other subconscious minds.

Substantially similar stories, some colored by highly imaginative reporting, appeared in scores of other newspapers up and down the country and as far west as the *Denver Post*. In California, where the blast had been triggered, the flurry was already past its peak.

While this storm was breaking, Edgar was placidly taking pictures for the Tressler Studio in Montgomery, and wondering how soon he and Gertrude would have enough money to go back into business for themselves.

His first knowledge of the tumult came from a reporter who tracked him down and handed him a sheaf of clippings from the newspapers. He was completely incredulous at first. Then, as he read the stories, he began to grow indignant. He had always been shy of publicity and faintly embarrassed when local papers wrote about

123

his power. Now, without as much as by-your-leave, his private life was being paraded before the whole country.

He was worried, too, over what effect this might have on his power. But most of all he was furious at Ketchum for using a medical reading to pry into a divergent subject without his permission, and without even telling him of it afterward. His old fears came back. He had almost forgotten how completely at the mercy of others he was during his hypnotic sleep. However true his own purpose might be when he lay down, a conductor could direct his power to any use he chose.

He was still in a turmoil when he heard from home. Gertrude and his mother described the invasion of reporters and the chaos that had resulted. Both were concerned for him, knowing how sensitive he was.

Then came a letter from Ketchum. He had organized a company to make use of Edgar's healing power. Besides himself, it included the squire and Albert Noe, owner of a Hopkinsville hotel and a man of substance. The fourth partner was to be Edgar, who was invited to name any terms he wanted for giving the readings.

Edgar's first reaction was outrage. Then gradually other thoughts filtered into his spinning brain. Was the idea after all so sacrilegious? If, as it appeared, God had somehow singled him out to possess the power to bring health and happiness to others, then would it not be serving His purpose to make that gift available to the greatest possible number of people? Edgar paced the floor through the night, wrestling with his doubts and fears. In the morning he sat down to answer Ketchum's letter.

He would accept the proposition on his own terms. No one but his father was ever to conduct a reading, and he was to remain on watch as long as Edgar was asleep. As an added safeguard, every word he spoke during a reading was to be taken down by a stenographer and two copies made, one for the patient and one for Edgar's files. He would give readings twice a day in a special office set up for the purpose, but only for the sick. Fees must be kept reasonable to all and waived in the case of any person in real need who lacked funds.

For his part, he flatly refused to take one penny that would be paid for the readings. But he did agree to let the company set him up in a modern photo studio with a minimum of $500 worth of equipment. He was to have a completely free hand to operate this as his own, and from the studio would come his only income.

He sent the letter north and a telegram sped back: WE ACCEPT. COME AT ONCE. MAIL PILING UP.

He reached Hopkinsville to find some ten thousand letters on hand from all parts of the country, with more pouring in each day. There were a number of crackpot missives, of course, but the majority were earnest pleas for help. From those he drew confidence in the rightness of his decision. His gift would be made available to the mass of people.

The newspaper stories had made no mention of fees, but many of the letters included offerings with the pitiful hope that the enclosure would be enough to bring help. There was more than $2,000 altogether, ranging from a crumpled dollar bill pinned to a sheet of cheap tablet paper to checks for sizable amounts.

"Send it back," Edgar said immediately. "We're not taking anyone's money until we're set up and ready to give them their reading."

His partners protested. They had every right to hold the money until he could get to the readings. Those who had not sent in enough could be billed for the balance. Edgar settled the matter by sitting down and personally returning the bulk of it. With every refund he included a personal note of thanks, explaining the delay and telling the sender how to reapply. The job gave him a deep satisfaction and a terrible case of writer's cramp.

Before the next step was taken, Edgar made a flat demand. "A lot of people, mostly doctors, accuse me of breaking the law by giving these readings. If I am doing that, I want to know it now, before I get in any deeper."

He had the squire invite a select group of judges and lawyers to witness a reading and give their opinions. The same question was put to the state medical association. The result was a unanimous decision that Edgar was violating no existing law.

Out of the opinions came a fact that startled Edgar. He was a man outside the law, or perhaps a law unto himself. Since no other person possessed his unique talent, any attempt to curb it would have to come through a special law aimed directly at him, which would be unconstitutional. It disturbed him a little to realize that even in the eyes of the law he was a freak.

With the way cleared, partnership papers were drawn up and the company became a reality. Upstairs offices were rented near the foot of Main Street. The photo studio would occupy the former census offices of Judge Anderson and an apartment directly across the hall was fitted out for the company's office and for the readings. A sign was painted on the door: *Edgar Cayce, Jr., Psychic Diagnostician.* The "Jr." was to avoid confusion with his uncle, Edgar Cayce.

His partners selected a letterhead that bore Edgar's picture, and furnishings that were on the bizarre side. They included a garish custom-made couch for the readings. Edgar was thankful that he had been given the $500 he specified and permitted to select his studio furnishings and equipment to his own more modest taste.

There was some wrangling over fees. Edgar wanted a small flat fee with each reading. The others held out for the method used by doctors, a final bill to cover additional check readings and any other incidental items. It was Edgar's suspicion that they wanted to follow the accepted medical practice in tailoring the final bill to match the patient's financial position. However, he was outnumbered and outvoted.

"I gave in," he told Gertrude wearily. "Maybe that way is the best, letting the rich ease the burden for the poor. But I keep seeing the cries for help come in and I can't stand more delay. I can't ask a dying man to hang onto life a little longer so we can quibble over details."

There was another argument which Edgar lost and which bothered his conscience for a long time afterward. He allowed himself to be sold on accepting payment for his readings.

The idea of accepting payment for his readings had always been repugnant to Edgar, but gradually his father and the others wore him down with logic and arguments. Gertrude finally tipped the scales.

"I think they're right, Edgar," she said one evening. "When the readings were just something you did as a personal help to someone, I felt the way you did, but the business setup has given me a different outlook."

"I don't even feel right about that," Edgar groaned. "It seems wrong to peddle a special gift through the mail, like one of those courses Layne was always taking."

"Remember the parable of the talents in the Bible, Edgar—the servant who buried his talent for fear of losing it was censured by the Lord. His blessing went to the one who used his talent and multiplied it. I'm sure that is what the Lord expects you to do with your great gift, to make it available to as many as possible. And now I'm sure He expects you to receive a fair wage for what you do. I've never seen anything in the Bible condemning fair pay or fair profit. If you'd become a minister as you wanted to, you would accept your salary without a thought."

Edgar threw up his hands in surrender. "All right, I'll do it. But it still doesn't seem right."

When he announced his agreement to accept a quarter of any net over expenses, the squire slapped him on the back. "Now you're getting sense, boy. I used to worry about those notions of yours. You've got the greatest gift in the world, son, but it's money makes the mare go."

All through the fall and early winter of 1910 Edgar put in long hours on the gaudy couch, working down through the piles of requests for readings. He was haunted by the slowness with which he could nibble into that mountain of need. The number of readings he could give without exhaustion was limited. The squire had become adept at halting each session before Edgar's strength was drained. No amount of argument would sway him on that point.

Every mail brought new requests, and almost every day people came to the office for personal readings. Over the protests of Gertrude and his father, Edgar began giving occasional extra evening readings in a vain effort to catch up. They tried, with no greater success, to keep him from reading the incoming mail. Appointments were piled up weeks ahead.

A reading was asked for a sick girl in Cleveland. When Edgar finally got to it and the diagnosis sent off, the answer came back, "Your diagnosis came too late to be useful. My daughter's condition grew so much worse that she was operated on three days ago. However, you may be interested to know that the surgeon found the condition of the organs exactly as the reading said they were."

"Send their money back," Edgar said wearily. "It's the least we can do."

Another worry began to pile its mounting weight on him. In almost every mail there were letters crying, "We can't find any doctor who will give the treatments you suggest. They say it's all a fake, or worse, and most of them won't even look at the reading. We're desperate."

There was nothing Edgar could do. Where he was personally known, the doctors were apt to show a grudging respect for his readings. Everywhere else they met scorn. Medical doctors were by far the most stubborn, despite the fact that Ketchum's paper had received widespread attention. Osteopaths were a little more ready to cooperate, but only when Edgar's diagnoses agreed with theirs.

"What can we do?" Edgar said to Gertrude, pacing the bedroom floor. "How can we get the treatments used, and used properly? Yesterday I took a check reading on a woman who wrote that the treatments were only making her worse. The reading said her doctor had substituted one of the ingredients in the prescription because it was cheaper, and he thought it was just as good. It happens all the time."

"I don't know anything you can do now," Gertrude said, "except to stop tearing yourself apart. You simply can't carry all the woes of the world on your shoulders

128

night and day. In God's good time, the answer will come."

The answer came very soon, although it took some time to recognize it and longer to put it into practice. It came in the person of a man named Mohr who owned a coal mine up at Nortonsville, Kentucky. Mohr wanted to meet Edgar personally and to obtain a reading for a niece who was crippled from infantile paralysis.

"I'm doing a mighty prosperous business, thanks to you," he told Edgar. "You're the one who discovered the coal mine I'm working."

Edgar stared at him. "I did? That's news to me."

"The man I bought it from said you did. You were working with a man named Layne then. He got Layne to ask you where a coal vein could be found and the reading gave the exact location. He dug, and there it was."

Edgar's lips tightened and his eyes glinted with anger. It was another instance where Layne had abused the power while Edgar was unconscious. But afterward, thinking it over, his resentment faded. Apparently the power had not resented being used for that purpose, for Edgar could remember no unpleasant reaction at that time. Perhaps it was right to use the readings for legitimate purposes other than healing.

Meanwhile he gave the reading on the little girl, and Mohr left with it. Some weeks later Mohr was back, bursting with enthusiasm. "You performed a miracle, Cayce. The doctors said she would never walk again, but last week she took her first steps."

"I'm glad," Edgar said, and his eyes glowed with pleasure.

Mohr's smile faded and his face darkened. "Damn those doctors. I had to scour the country and practically threaten with a gun to get one who'd even look at your reading. Then it took another battle to make him follow the treatment you outlined. He saw her walk, but he still says you're a fake."

"I know," Edgar said gloomily. "We get that all the time, and there isn't a thing we can do about it."

"The hell there isn't," Mohr barked. "That's exactly

why I'm here. I want to buy out those partners of yours and move you to Nortonsville. The answer to the problem is a hospital, staffed with every kind of doctor your readings might call for, ones who will follow your treatments properly, down to the last detail. People who can't get cooperation from doctors at home can go to the hospital and get what they need. That's what you need, Cayce, and I want to build and equip it for you."

Chapter Sixteen

"YOU SAID we'd find the answer eventually, and this is it," Edgar told Gertrude exultantly. "We'll have our own hospital, where we can give people everything they need to get well."

"It sounds wonderful," Gertrude said, "but will you be able to arrange it? I know your father will approve, but what about Noe and Ketchum? Will they let you go?"

Edgar admitted, "You should have heard the howl when Mohr told them he wanted to buy them out. They argued all afternoon. Mohr finally left for Nortonsville. He's coming back in a week or so to see if they've changed their minds."

The argument raged on while Edgar walked in a golden dream. He began to envision a string of hospitals across the country, within easy reach of everyone. He could give the readings from a central headquarters, then send the patient to the nearest hospital for treatment to be carried out. It would enormously multiply the good he could do.

Mohr returned to be met by an exorbitant price on the deal. After more argument, he made a counteroffer and gave them more time to think it over. To Edgar he confided privately, "They'll come around eventually. I'm so sure of it that I've already started building your hospital. The basement's dug and the foundation half finished right now. It won't be long."

Edgar's spirits soared higher as Noe and Ketchum began to weaken.

Then Mohr came back, but not to conclude a deal. He was carried in; he had been injured in a mine acci-

131

dent, and his only interest now was in obtaining a reading that would tell how to ease his pain and mend his broken body. He got the reading, but when no doctor in Nortonsville would even consider giving the treatment it called for, he went back to his home in Ohio. While he slowly recuperated, the mine got into difficulties. His fortune slipped away, and with it Edgar's hospital.

Edgar was sick with disappointment, but now he had a goal to strive for. Somehow, some place, he would eventually have such a hospital. Of that he was sure.

In March, 1911, the Hearst newspapers ran a series of illustrated pieces on Edgar and his miracle readings. These aroused such interest that the Hearst organization invited Edgar and his father to spend two weeks in Chicago to give a series of readings before a group of leading medical men.

Edgar longed to see the great city, but when he looked at the fresh torrents of mail begging for medical readings, he shook his head.

"I think you should go," Gertrude told him. "You need the rest and the change. But even more important, if you can show some of the most famous doctors in the country that what you're doing is sound and right, it will help break down the resistance of the whole profession. In the long run, it might help more people than if you stay here."

Her logic convinced Edgar and he accepted. He was properly awed by the size of Chicago and the magnificence of the bridal suite reserved for them at the Palmer House. This turned out to be the only pleasant memory of the trip. Everything else resulted in frustration and fury.

From the moment they stepped off the train they were badgered by cynical reporters and gaped at by curious crowds. Edgar's temper flared when he discovered that bellboys at the hotel were charging five dollars to snatch open his door so guests could get a look at the freak from Kentucky.

Edgar was confronted with the most outrageous demands for demonstrations. No one had bothered to learn exactly what the nature of his psychic power was, so he was asked to do magic, to bring back spirits of the dead, to levitate an elephant, and perform other stunts even more ridiculous.

The mysterious disappearance of Dorothy Arnold was then in the news. One brash reporter sidled up. "We've got it all set for you, bud. You're going to pull one of your trances at the biggest theater in town and tell the crowd what happened to the Arnold girl."

When Edgar refused to participate in any stunts or public demonstrations, the reporters took their revenge by running stories adverse to him. There were fake interviews in which he was supposed to have made fantastic claims for his mystic powers, and then to have offered nothing but weak excuses and lame alibis when they demanded proof.

The only comforting note in this brazen clamor was an afternoon paper that ran an accurate, uncolored description of his readings.

Meanwhile the plan to demonstrate before doctors was deteriorating into an even worse debacle. The first group invited—the leading physicians and surgeons of the city—flatly refused even to attend and issued statements that they would have nothing whatever to do with such nonsense.

After several days a handful of lesser lights in the profession had reluctantly agreed out of curiosity to witness a reading. But when Edgar insisted on their giving an honest statement of their opinions afterward, they refused, and left hastily.

Arrangements had been made to give the reading for a woman who was dangerously ill from an ailment that had not yet been diagnosed. Edgar was determined to give her reading, with or without witnesses. At the last moment, one of the doctors decided he would sit in just to see what it was all about. A public stenographer was brought in and a Hearst reporter joined the doctor as a witness.

Edgar lay down and put himself to sleep, the squire conducting the reading. When he awoke, the stenographer was gone and his father was livid with rage. "The damn, insolent puppy! Right after you had started the diagnosis he jumped up and slammed his notebook shut. He said he couldn't take down such gibberish and he wasn't going to hang around and listen to the ravings of a lunatic."

Edgar sat glumly, then looked at the doctor, who seemed to be in a daze. "Did I give anything to help that poor woman? You would know if what I said made sense, Doctor."

"Remarkable," the doctor mumbled. "Remarkable."

The reporter whipped out a pencil. "May I quote you?"

The doctor came out of his daze with a bellow. "Don't you dare, young man. If you mention my name in your paper, or even hint that I attended this . . . . this *seance,* I'll sue you for slander. Why, I'd be laughed out of the medical association."

As he stalked to the door, Edgar called, "But you will see that the woman is given the benefit of whatever help there was in the reading, won't you? You can examine her and find out if the diagnosis was right, and give her the treatments."

The doctor looked back. "Do you think I'm crazy?"

"Come on, Dad," Edgar said, getting to his feet. "I've had all I can stand. We're taking the next train home."

The experience left bitterness. He plunged back into the readings with a frantic urgency to reach more people. There were letters of gratitude pouring in to lift his gloom, and other letters of despair to bring it back. *The doctor says we must be crazy. The doctor won't even read your diagnosis. The doctor says he won't even answer a call from anyone who would listen to a spiritualist fake.* A hundred cases paraded across the screen of memory. Where would Carrie be today, or chubby little Tom House, Jr., or the Dietrich girl, if doctors had the final word?

On March 29th Gertrude presented him with a new son, Milton Porter Cayce. Edgar's mercurial spirits shot skyward again. He was a father, with his own miracles humbled by the greater miracle that wailed in Gertrude's arms.

The baby was sick and cried all the time, and Gertrude was badly worried. Edgar comforted her and rushed back to the readings with no real concern. He remembered how Hugh Lynn had cried endlessly during his first months, and now no one ever saw a plumper, healthier four-year-old.

He was stunned when the doctor told him Milton Porter Cayce was dying. "It went into colitis and God knows what all. We've done all we can, but he's so small and frail. He has no strength and no resistance."

Edgar jumped up wildly. "Where is my father? Get him over here fast. I've got to give a reading. Oh, why didn't I give it before?"

He awoke from the reading and knew the answer without asking. He could read it in his father's haggard face, in Gertrude's wracking sobs. He got up off the couch and left the house, tears streaming down his own cheeks. In that mysterious hour before dawn, when all life reaches its lowest ebb, the baby died—the reading had said it would.

The question haunted his waking moments and came back in his dreams. "Why didn't I take a reading the very first day he took sick? Don't I trust my own power? Why didn't Gertrude ask for a reading? Doesn't she trust it, either?"

He tramped the fields and woods alone, tortured by grief and the terrible, wrenching question—could an earlier reading have saved his son? He opened his Bible and a phrase leaped out at him: *Oh, ye of little faith* . . . He put his face down into his hands and wept.

With the death of her baby something went out of Gertrude. Day by day she grew more pale and listless. For long hours she would sit, staring dully into space, neither speaking nor heeding anything around her. Edgar thought she was being consumed by grief and virtually gave up the photo studio to spend more time at home, trying to comfort her.

She caught a cold, and it developed into pleurisy that dragged on and sapped her fading strength. Now Edgar was frantic to get a reading on her, but he delayed, wanting her to ask him for it. By asking, she would show her faith in his power. It never occurred to him that she was simply too ill to ask anything.

With terrible suddenness Dr. Jackson, the family physician, summoned him. "I hope you can take a bad shock, Edgar. I've had specialists in to confirm a suspicion about Gertrude. She has tuberculosis in an advanced stage. She's hemorrhaging now, and we can't stop it. She may or may not last out the week. I see no hope unless you can find something in that business you do in your sleep."

Edgar sprang out of his daze. "My father's at the studio. I'll take a reading right away."

The specialists were there with Doctors Jackson and Ketchum, and a local pharmacist. The minister who had married them had heard of the reading and arrived, bringing the Methodist minister to add the power of prayer to the power within Edgar. They were praying when Edgar put himself to sleep.

When he opened his eyes, his first words were, "Will she live?"

"Yes," the squire said, and squeezed Edgar's shoulder. "You said she would."

The doctors were arguing violently over the weird conglomeration of treatments that had poured out of him. He had called for heroin, compounded with other drugs and administered in capsules. He was wrong right there, they told him, for heroin simply would not compound as he specified. Osteopathic adjustments to the spine sounded plain ridiculous for a bacterial infection of the lungs. As for that last prescription—that was sheer fantasy, straight out of whatever twisted dream world his subconscious had wandered in while he slept.

"Take a charred oak keg," his voice had told them, "of a gallon and a half capacity. Put into it one gallon of pure apple brandy and inhale the fumes from it four times daily."

The specialists offered their condolences and left. The pharmacist looked hard at Dr. Ketchum. "Do you write a prescription for that heroin or do I go to jail for dispensing narcotics without a prescription? I've never known one of Edgar's readings to be wrong yet."

"I'll write it," Ketchum said, a little grimly. "But damn it, the heroin *won't* compound."

It was quite a while before Edgar got around to recording the balance of the story in his diary. "The medicine *did* compound and with the first dose of this there were no more hemorrhages—but perhaps she wasn't going to have any more anyhow. The next day there was no fever—but possibly the fever had already broken. I don't know."

It was not lack of faith now that made him qualify each triumph. Throughout his life he had a horror of claiming credit for any cure that might already have begun through natural processes. Later, when more detailed records were being kept, he insisted that same attitude be applied to every report.

One time he was giving a reading for a woman who had become stone deaf. As he awoke, he heard her cry to her husband, "I heard him. I heard every word that man said, and I can hear everything now. He cured me by a miracle."

Edgar sat up, shaking his head. "The miracle wasn't mine. Your deafness must have been due to something in your own mind. You cured yourself, and I can take no credit." Afterward he saw to it that this explanation was written on the record and he forbade anyone to publicize the case or point it out as an example of his power.

Meanwhile Gertrude made slow but unmistakable progress, set back by colds as winter closed in, but always moving toward restored health. That winter Dr. Hugo Munsterberg came out from Harvard University to expose Edgar Cayce as a fake. He studied the readings that charted Gertrude's return from the edge of death. He pumped the Dietrichs and half a dozen other families where Edgar's power had restored someone to health. He witnessed a reading and went away, shaking his head, mumbling, "It is not good to believe things

137

that are against science and reason, but what else can I do?"

Winter bludgeoned the town with cold and snow. The squire slipped on ice and broke his kneecap. While he was laid up, Edgar faced the alternative of giving up the readings for weeks or going ahead without the squire to act as conductor. He looked at the mountain of mail and made his reluctant decision.

"I'll go ahead," he told Ketchum, "but I want the full transcript of every word spoken, so I can check it."

The readings proceeded on this understanding, but one day there was no stenographer to take down his words. Ketchum explained, with some embarrassment, "We're not getting the money in as we should. You're giving too many free readings and you argue every time we want to put on pressure for uncollected bills. We can't afford to pay a stenographer the way things are at the moment. I can take notes myself and write out the treatments afterward."

Edgar wasn't happy, but he knew Ketchum was right about finances. He went on with the readings, afterward glancing over the notes, which had little meaning for him anyhow.

Then he began to awaken, feeling tired and strangely depressed. The old headaches came back, and with them a growing suspicion. He remembered how he always felt when he answered questions which had nothing to do with medical readings.

Armed with his suspicions, Edgar confronted Dr. Ketchum.

The doctor chewed his lip. "Look, Edgar," he said finally, "you've got to face up to a few realities. In your sleep, you're a man of miracles. Awake, you're an impractical visionary. You want to help more people, and we want to make that possible. We want the same thing you do—help for people in need, a hospital to ensure their getting the right treatments, the respect of scientific authorities. But how are we going to get them?"

"What *did* you ask in those readings?"

Ketchum's jaw set. "About ways to raise money to help us. You've never made fullest use of that gift of yours. We talked it over and decided it wouldn't hurt to keep you in the dark a while and try to accomplish some things you refuse to do for yourself."

Edgar sighed and tossed a key onto the desk. "I'm sorry. I know you meant well. You always have. Maybe I am a sort of fool for not being more practical. I don't know. But I do know I have to have someone I can trust when I'm asleep. Like Layne, you meant to help, but I can't give myself and my power in your hands any longer. Here's the key to your studio."

He turned and stumbled out, ignoring Ketchum's anxious call. There were always jobs for photographers in Alabama.

Chapter Seventeen

CAYCE WENT FIRST TO Montgomery, Alabama, to the Tressler Studio, where he had been working when Ketchum's story got him into the headlines. They had told him then there would always be a job for him if he wanted it. Now they wanted him to open and manage a branch studio in Selma, on shares. It prospered from the start. When the hospital liked his X-rays and offered him a job, he worked it out on a part-time basis so he could manage the studio afternoons and evenings, and do X-ray work each morning.

He liked Selma, Alabama, at first sight. To Gertrude he wrote, "I can hardly wait until you're strong enough to travel. You'll love it here, and prospects are wonderful. I've been offered an unbelievable salary to take X-ray pictures for the hospital, and I've accepted. I'll be helping the sick that way and I can forget about the readings. They've brought us misery too often and so few people are helped because doctors refuse to give the treatments."

One of the first friends he made there was Ed Williamson, Selma freight agent for the Southern Railway. Ed was intensely interested in hypnotism and liked to talk about it, but Edgar always changed the subject. No one in Selma had associated him with the "illiterate psychic diagnostician" of the newspaper stories, and he meant to keep it that way. His only link with the past was a few regular check readings for Gertrude and for a handful of earlier patients whose recovery would take time. Gertrude's brother, Lynn, who was working in nearby Anniston, came over weekends to conduct these.

The rest of the week Cayce wanted to keep psychic diagnoses completely out of his mind.

After a few months of booming business he had enough money to buy out the Tressler interest and hang a new sign out over Broad Street—*Cayce Studio*. He announced his ownership of the studio, expecting floods of business. Instead he got floods of rain. Day after dreary day the torrents poured down, drowning the crops in the fields, wrecking bridges, making roads impassable. Farmers could not get in to have pictures taken, even if they could have afforded the extravagance.

Edgar's situation was desperate and he was frantic. Was bad luck to dog him all his days? Was this a punishment for having broken with Ketchum and Noe who, in spite of what happened, had been the only ones to make his power available to the greatest number of people?

The day after he had spent his last dollar for food, he sat in the studio, praying for guidance. He needed money to live on, but even more he needed some sign to point out his path. Suddenly he heard the downstairs door slam.

A woman came into the studio. Her face was wrinkled, her hands work-worn. She wore the shabby-clean garments of respectable poverty which held no promise of business for Edgar.

To his surprise she drew out a tintype of a smiling boy. "Could you make a real picture from this? It is my only son. He is so far away, in Alaska, and I want his picture to put up where I can look at it."

"I'm sure I can," Edgar said, studying the tintype with an expert eye. "It hasn't faded too much, yet." He named a price far lower than he would normally ask.

Her face lighted, then fell. "But I can't pay you until I can get a check cashed. My boy sent it, but because it is from so far off, nobody will cash it for me."

Edgar looked at the check, drawn on a bank in Alaska. "If you'll wait, I'll see if I can get it cashed for you."

At the bank the cashier looked at the check and grimaced. "That one again. This is the third time it's been in here today. I've turned it down before, but for you I'll take a chance."

"I haven't anything in my account to cover it," Edgar said.

The cashier grinned. "If I'm going to worry about anybody's honesty, Cayce, it won't be yours. Here's the money."

When Edgar returned, the woman burst into tears. She had spent her last cent coming into town. She had walked the streets, frightened and bewildered, until something impelled her to turn in at the studio door. "I don't know what I would have done. My daughter is home alone and she is crippled from infantile paralysis."

"Crippled?" Edgar repeated. He looked down at the money in his hand, given him to pay for copying the tintype. "Could you bring her in here tomorrow? It is possible I might be able to help her walk normally again."

When she had gone, he lifted his eyes and whispered quite simply, "Thank you, God, for the sign." Then he went down to the freight office to give Ed Williamson the shock of his life.

Ed conducted the reading the next day, still awed by the revelation of Edgar's identity. In lieu of a stenographer, Dr. Gay, a physician whose office was nearby, was asked to sit in. He studied Edgar's clippings without comment and agreed to listen to the reading and interpret the diagnosis and suggestions. He sat with a wooden, expressionless face that revealed nothing of his thoughts. When Edgar awoke, that face was still expressionless, but Gay said quietly, "The diagnosis was sound and the treatment, while unorthodox, seems reasonable. I'll give the treatments myself." He looked at the woman, and at the girl with the crippled leg. "There will be no charge."

In a month the leg was stronger and straighter. Within a year it was normal and the girl could walk without a limp.

Meanwhile Gay got a reading that cleared up a disfiguring sore on his father's face. He never volunteered an opinion on psychic diagnosis, and Edgar never asked for one.

From the day of the girl's reading, Edgar's fortunes improved. The rains ceased and studio business came back. He got the joyous news that Gertrude would be strong enough to join him late that summer of 1913. As word of his strange gift was spread, he began to give regular readings, with Ed Williamson as his enthusiastic conductor.

During this period, he became an ardent and skillful canner of fruits and vegetables. Later Gertrude came to view the hobby with reserve. In time of great emotional stress, Edgar was apt to plunge into an orgy of canning that had every cabinet and closet in the house overflowing with jars.

Everything finally seemed to be going well, now that Gertrude and Hugh Lynn were with him at last, when one night Ed Williamson dropped into the studio grinning. "Brace yourself, boy. You don't know it yet, but you're famous."

Edgar looked up quickly. "What do you mean?" He listened with set jaw and smoldering eyes to the story Ed gleefully unfolded.

It had started when Ed noticed a publicity item in a newspaper. Carl Laemmle, president of Universal Films, announced a search for scenarios important enough to be starring vehicles for some of his rising young actors and actresses.

The item sparked a flash of genius in Ed's mind.

He wrote Laemmle a letter describing Edgar's power, and enclosing some of the earlier newspaper clippings. Describing himself as Edgar's intimate friend and assistant, he said, "If you are interested and will write me, naming a date and the hour, allowing for the difference in time—one hour—stating the name of the party you have in mind to take the lead in a movie, and exactly where she will be, I think I can surprise you."

Laemmle immediately saw the possibilities for a beautiful publicity stunt and turned the letter over to Nat Rothstein, head of publicity and advertising for

Universal, who contacted Ed. It had originally been Ed's intention to let Edgar in on the deal when it was all set. At the last moment his nerve wavered and he convinced himself it would be better to surprise Edgar with a fait accompli.

Meanwhile Nat Rothstein was issuing mysterious invitations and carefully building curiosity with veiled references to a seance, and something he glibly called a psychoscenario. As an added hook, the guests were to share this mystery with Violet Mersereau, a young star whom Laemmle was trying to build into the pin-up queen of 1913.

On a Thursday night, thirty reporters' and trade journal representatives gathered at Churchill's, in New York. Violet was a charming and agreeable hostess. When everyone was settled, Rothstein mounted a rostrum to tell about Edgar, whose name he mispronounced as Case. He described Ed Williamson's offer, and then held up a sheet of paper covered with writing.

"We have here a detailed account of what Miss Mersereau considers the perfect type of story for her next starring picture. No one has read it but Miss Mersereau and the stenographer. At precisely eight-thirty, this will be placed face up in the exact center of the small table you see here on the platform. It will remain there for fifty minutes. During that time, while Edgar Cayce is in a trance, it is claimed that his spirit will fly here, read the details of what Miss Mersereau wants, then fly back to dictate a perfect psychoscenario to fill those needs." The sheet was solemnly placed on the table.

In Selma, Edgar arranged himself on the couch for a reading. As usual, he had not bothered to ask anything about it; he had come to trust Ed completely. When he awoke, Ed hurried off to write up his rough notes. . . .

"Do you know what you really did that night, Edgar?" Ed demanded now. "You read that paper in New York and you dictated a scenario that just filled the bill. The title on it was 'Through The Sublimal.' The New York papers played it up big. Violet Mersereau said it was exactly what she wanted, and they turned it

144

over to the scenario editor. When your psychic movie comes out, nobody'll ever say your power is a fake."

"I'm sorry, Ed," Edgar said quietly. "I trusted you and you tricked me. It doesn't matter how innocent or worthwhile your purpose might be—you weren't honest with me. You'll never conduct another reading of any kind." He went heavily up the stairs to the apartment.

Upstairs he held Gertrude close and poured out the story. "What can I do? How can I go on taking readings? There's no one I can trust." He stopped suddenly, a strange expression dawning on his face. "There's one person I could trust always. I could trust you. Gertrude, would—would you consider conducting my readings?"

She smiled tenderly and kissed him. "I've been waiting a long time for you to ask me."

Chapter Eighteen

WITH GERTRUDE conducting the readings, Edgar no longer faced them with dread. With the weight lifted from his mind, he began to think more objectively about his power. He and Gertrude had long talks about its potentialities. Unknowingly, he was preparing himself for the next great step.

A lumberman from Lexington sent him a check for expenses and insisted Edgar visit him to see for himself what one of his readings had wrought on his arthritic wife. Edgar went, and stood choked with emotion as the woman showed him how, for the first time in many years, she could raise her arms high enough to comb her own hair.

"While you're here," the lumberman said, "I'd like you to give a reading for one of our neighbors. They're the Solomon Kahns, one of the nicest families you'll ever meet. One of their sons has been ailing for some time."

Edgar's reading for the boy revealed a simple difficulty that began to clear up at once. He felt himself immensely drawn to the Kahns and especially to eighteen-year-old David, the eldest. They were deeply religious people with his own kind of simple, unshakable faith in God. Edgar spent long, comfortable evenings with them.

"You were telling about other information besides medical that has come out of readings," young Dave said thoughtfully one night. "I'm wondering why you couldn't give some sort of vocational readings, telling people not only about their health but about their minds and souls as well. You suggest treatments for healing sick bodies; why can't you suggest treatments that will heal sick minds and spirits and mend broken or wasted lives?"

"Oh, I don't think so," Edgar said, startled. "That's getting into something a little too deep."

"I'll bet you could," Dave said.

His mother nodded. "God walks beside Edgar Cayce. There is nothing he cannot do to help others."

He tried to dismiss the idea, but it began to send out roots. His last evening in Lexington he let Dave conduct a reading on himself. In addition to checking on the boy's physical condition, they worked out a few simple test questions designed to learn how far the power might go in helping him plan his life.

When Edgar awoke they were staring at him with wondering eyes. Dave said, "You can add the gift of prophecy to your list of miracles. You told me a lot of things about how I should live and conduct myself. Then you told me I was going to leave home and find success in a line of work I'm not trained for and have never even thought of. You said my family would object to my leaving but that I should go anyhow, because that move would affect my whole life. And you said I was going to have a great deal to do with helping your work in the future, but I'd already made up my mind to that."

Edgar blurted, "I just remembered something. Back when I started with Ketchum and Noe in Hopkinsville, they asked in a reading if the company would succeed. The answer was that my work would find its greatest success when there was a Jew associated with it."

"Maybe I'm that Jew," Dave said soberly.

They shook hands on it solemnly, while Dave's parents beamed.

Back in Selma he told Gertrude all about his visit and about Dave's idea of life readings. She nodded. "I think he's right, Edgar. I've always had a feeling that your gift was meant to do more than just cure ailments. We must give it a lot of thought and try some experiments to see exactly what a reading can do."

Before they could carry out this intention, tragedy struck again. Playing around the studio on a cold day in

147

February, young Hugh Lynn came upon a stock of his father's flash powder. He had always been fascinated watching Edgar pour the gray magnesium into its trough, hold it over his head, and pull the ring that struck sparks from flint and steel. He had been warned not to look directly at the blinding flash but he always did, and then minutes would pass before he could see again.

Now he saw the fascinating powder and a box of matches, and temptation was too great. He heaped a big pile on the floor, knelt with his face over it, and struck a match.

In the darkroom, Edgar felt the soft concussion and heard the terrible, piercing shriek of agony. When he ran out, Hugh Lynn was on hands and knees, the screams pouring out of the blackened horror that had been his face. Edgar caught him up and ran.

The eye specialists shook their heads gravely. "There's no point in building up false hopes. We see very little chance of saving his sight. In fact, one eye is so badly damaged that it must be removed at once if we're to save his life."

Hugh Lynn clung to his father, sobbing wildly. Edgar set his jaw grimly. "You'll do nothing until I've taken a reading. And I insist on your being present to interpret and follow any treatment that may be recommended."

The doctors exchanged looks and then shrugged. They had heard rumors of Edgar's uncanny power and had been wryly amused at the ridiculous things some people would believe.

"All right," one said, "if it will make you feel better."

Never had Gertrude revealed her inner strength more clearly than in the calmness with which she conducted the reading. When Edgar awoke, the doctors were staring at him oddly. "For a man who isn't supposed to know medicine, you speak with a lot of authority. You said if the boy were kept in a dark room for fifteen days, with dressings soaked in strong tannic acid kept on his eyes and changed at frequent intervals, his sight would be restored. Why, that might cause irreparable damage to the delicate tissues of the eye."

"To which eye?" Edgar asked flatly. "The one you say is already beyond hope, or the one you intended to remove anyhow?"

There was no answer to that. They prepared the solution and put on the dressing. During the longest fifteen days of anguish in their lives, Edgar and Gertrude waited and prayed. The doctors changed the dressings, puzzled because Hugh Lynn suffered no pain at all, and because the eye they had wanted to remove caused no trouble whatever.

At last the ordeal was over. The final dressing came away; the face underneath was clear, the faint tracery of scar tissue almost invisible. The eyes were bright and sparkling.

"I can see," Hugh Lynn cried joyfully. "I can see everything just as good as I could before." He hugged his parents, wondering at their tears; he had never before seen his father cry.

They were busy and happy in Selma. Church work and the readings brought them hosts of friends. Edgar's Sunday School class was a great success. The place was so deeply rooted in their lives that they were disturbed when a reading said, in response to a question about Edgar's dream of a hospital, "This will happen when you are near the water. It is best for your work to be beside the ocean, to have people come to you across water. The best place for you to be is Virginia Beach, in Virginia."

No one had ever heard of Virginia Beach. Eventually a man who had done considerable traveling recalled it as a tiny fishing village somewhere around Norfolk. The idea held no allure for Edgar and Gertrude; they loved Selma and were helping a great many people.

Another matter disturbed them greatly. A reading said that the war boiling up in Europe would spread across the world and embroil America. Hordes of fine young men would never return from the fields of Flanders. They talked of this between themselves, and agreed that the gift of prophecy was not the blessing it might seem. To know of an impending horror and be

149

powerless to avert it laid a monstrous weight on the human mind. . . .

During this period Edgar learned another fact about the immensity of his power. Members of his early Sunday School classes had gone out to far corners of the earth as missionaries. Letters with curious stamps began to come in, asking readings for people with strange names and unpronounceable addresses.

Edgar was dubious, but willing to try. Afterward he was stunned when Gertrude told him he had diagnosed the condition of a sick woman in a village in India as swiftly and easily as a patient in his own waiting room. From that milestone, his readings became global in scope.

About this time he began to startle Gertrude by injecting odd little side comments into the readings, remarks that showed clearly that some inner vision actually reached out to the place where the patient waited. Some were puzzling, some amusing.

Reading for a woman hundreds of miles away whom he had never seen, he began, "Yes, we have the body. Rather stout, with a pinched nose. A has-been blonde." Of a man in California, he said, "Not bad-looking pajamas." The patient later wrote, confirming the fact he had donned new bright red pajamas for the reading. On another occasion Edgar remarked, "Yes, in the gents' room. We have the body here." His yearning to travel gave him a sharp eye for details. "Sivas, Turkey—what a quaint place." Another time: "Penn Street, Denver, Colorado. We can get a view of the dome from here."

Some of the remarks were puzzling. Reading on a man in England, he began, "What funny little bungalows." At the end of the reading he added thoughtfully, "We do not find it best for the entity to return to the region of the peculiar-looking huts." Long afterward they learned that the man was a missionary from the Belgian Congo whose health had broken down from the jungle climate.

Edgar was as startled at these asides as Gertrude had been. They were unmistakable evidence that he was strongly clairvoyant. He had shown occasional clairvoyance in the past, but seldom in a physical reading. Now it was almost as if his power were deliberately forcing this talent to the fore. They discussed it often and agreed that psychic diagnosis was using only a small fraction of the total ability that was his to command.

They talked about Dave Kahn's idea of vocational readings and acknowledged their potential value, but Edgar found himself reluctant to begin. He flinched from the thought of tampering with people's lives as he had first flinched from the thought of tampering with their bodies. He sensed that he was being driven to it, but he put it off as long as he could.

Chapter Nineteen

DAVE KAHN wrote frequently. Then, after a long silence, came a letter full of excitement. "Chalk up another score for your readings. I was suddenly offered a good job with a furniture manufacturer out of town. My folks raised a fuss because they'd always figured my bent was toward clothing or textiles. I was dubious myself, but I remembered what your reading said. I took the job and discovered furniture is my field. They just gave me a nice promotion and said I had a real future."

Edgar put down the letter and stared out the window. Hugh Lynn and some of his friends raced by below. How differently their lives might turn out if they could know in their formative youth what field of endeavor would best use their natural talents. He would certainly take a life reading on Hugh Lynn—one of these days.

A few days later his voice faded and then died to a whisper.

When Gertrude got ready to conduct his self-treatment, he found he could not put himself into his hypnotic sleep. For a week they tried each day without result. Edgar's panic grew.

Dr. Gay could find nothing to help among his medicines, but he knew doctors who were experimenting with hypnotism in suggestive therapeutics. They tried earnestly, but no one could get Edgar into the third hypnotic stage where he would take the necessary posthypnotic suggestion. They decided it would probably take some kind of strong shock to bring his voice back.

The next night fire broke out in the store underneath the studio and apartment. Edgar started out of sleep in a room thick with smoke. He sprang up in wild terror, trying to shout at Gertrude to awaken and flee while he ran for Hugh Lynn. All the sound he could utter was the same thin whisper. Shock apparently was not the cure, either.

Fortunately the fire was put out before the upstairs quarters were damaged, but Edgar was too deep in despair to be glad.

A few days later a friend of Edgar's, an employee of the local gas company and an ardent student of hypnotism, came into the studio. "I've done a lot of thinking about your case, Edgar, and I've come up with an idea that might possibly work. If you'll let me try it, it can't possibly do any harm."

Edgar assented dully and Gertrude came to watch. The friend put him as far under as he would go, then began to talk quietly. "You love to hunt. You're out hunting now with your gun and dogs. You're crossing a big field, hoping your dogs will flush some birds. There's another hunter walking along over to your right." He suddenly raised his voice. "Look out! Your dogs are running in front of that other man's gun. Better call them back fast."

Edgar sat up, gave a piercing whistle, and shouted, "Get back here, you brutes! Heel! Heel!"

When Edgar was awakened, his voice was strong and normal.

"I think," Gertrude said quietly, that evening, "you'd better get started on life readings."

"I guess I'll have to," Edgar said helplessly. . . .

They began to experiment with vocational readings, but the results were disappointing. Answers were often vague or ambiguous. "We're not asking the right questions," Edgar said, "or not asking them in the right way."

"Either that," Gertrude said, "or we're simply not going into it deeply enough."

While they worried, the physical readings went on, but with a new element of uncertainty. For no reason that they could fathom, Edgar began to hit periods when he could not put himself to sleep, sometimes for days at a time. Or he would hypnotize himself and sleep for an hour or more without uttering a word or taking any suggestions except the one to awaken. Once or twice he suddenly awoke without suggestion, before Gertrude could finish reading the name and address of a patient.

"I think you're working too hard and wearing yourself down with worry," Gertrude said. "The power is forcing you to rest, just the way it did those other times, only not so drastically."

He tried to agree, but he could not keep himself from the terrifying thought that his gift was gradually fading away as his voice so often had. Then an incident occurred that heartened him, for he took it as a direct sign. . . .

After a particularly successful period, he lay down to try one reading that was badly needed. He got this easily. Then, instead of his customary closing, "We are through for the present," he went rushing on into another diagnosis. Before he stopped talking he had given eight more.

He awoke to find Gertrude staring dazedly at her notes. She told him what he had done. He was jubilant. "I'm sure that's a sign that you were right. Now that I'm rested, maybe I'll be able to catch up."

"I suppose so," she said helplessly, "but that isn't the point. We don't have requests for these other readings. I've never even heard of these names."

They were baffled until the mail came. In it were requests for five of those eight mysterious readings. The next mail held the other three.

"How did I do it?" Edgar asked numbly. "How did I know those people had letters in the mail asking for readings, and how did I know what the requests said? Usually, to give a reading for someone who isn't right here, I have to have that person in a special place at a special time, and I have to know exactly how to find that place. Then I do something like this. The more I use my power, the less I understand it."

"I believe you're growing," Gertrude said, "expanding your gift. I'm sure you can do things now that you couldn't have done back in Hopkinsville."

War came, as prophesied. An influential friend was

going to get Dave Kahn a commission. Edgar took a reading that said the attempt would fail. "Enlist in the regular way," it added. "You will be placed in a branch of the service where you will give the greatest service and be the happiest, and will earn your commission. Wherever you are stationed you should make every effort to arrange entertainment for the troops."

Dave enlisted, and every detail of the reading came true. After the war was over, he returned from France, a captain by merit, with many friends made from his unselfish extra project of bringing entertainment to the troops.

While so many of his younger friends were at war, Edgar celebrated his fortieth birthday by again becoming a father. Another son, Edgar Evans Cayce, was born on February 9, 1918. Edgar kept an anxious watch this time, ready for a reading at the first indication of a sniffle, but the baby was sound and healthy.

He was giving more readings than ever. His fame was spreading. Soldiers going out from Selma carried the story of his work to new parts of the world. More and more requests for readings began to come in from foreign countries.

Dave Kahn told the story of Edgar Cayce to an Italian consul while abroad. The consul carried it home and presently Edgar was staring in bewilderment at a letter written in Italian, on the impressive stationery of the Italian royal family. He finally took it down to an Italian fruit peddler for translation.

The peddler looked at the letter and was almost rendered speechless by his awe. A man who bought fruit from him was being petitioned for medical help by a member of Italian royalty. He was so impressed that Edgar invited him to attend the reading.

Gertrude gave the opening suggestion, stumbling a little over the strange name and address. Edgar began to talk rapidly and the peddler shot to his feet, wild with excitement. This reading was pouring out of Edgar's mouth in fluent and flawless Italian. Gertrude halted him with the suggestion that the reading be given in English. He switched immediately and began again in his normal manner and language.

The peddler went away, shaking his head in wonder. He bothered Edgar for a long time by insisting on speaking Italian whenever Edgar stopped to buy fruit.

Some time later part of a Cuban reading came out in perfect Spanish, but was hastily corrected to English. There were a few other instances of "speaking with tongues," but they were rare. Apparently the power, like Edgar himself, had an aversion to the dramatic.

The war years brought many changes in Edgar and in his use of the gift within him. As it expanded, so did his acceptance by the public. Sometimes he and Gertrude would be stunned by the names that showed up in their daily mail. One of America's top steel magnates, a leading automobile manufacturer, a U. S. Senator, a famous movie producer, a leading Hollywood actress, heads of a dozen major industries—these turned to Edgar Cayce for help.

On two occasions during the frenzy of World War I, Edgar was mysteriously summoned to Washington. Both trips were surrounded by a veil of secrecy that was never lifted.

The development of this new type of reading grew naturally out of the chaos of war. People harassed by doubts and fears begged Edgar to turn his power to world conditions.

"I don't think I should," he protested to Gertrude. "I'm not even sure my gift would operate in a big field like that. What do I know about things like economics and world politics?"

"What do you know about medicine?" she challenged. "I think you should try the readings. For a long time now your power has been showing evidence of knowledge far beyond merely diagnosing illness. Remember what a reading told us the other day?"

Edgar nodded, quoting, "It would be wrong to save this body and not save the soul." He paced nervously, twisting his hands. "That seems reasonable. But I can't see a connection between man's soul and—and whether the Allies will hold back the Boches."

"It seems to me there's a very intimate connection, Edgar. Man's soul is his own, but at the same time it is also one with all the other souls in the universe. All souls, working together in harmony or disharmony, make world conditions. Sick souls cause a sick world."

"Well, I'll try," Edgar said doubtfully. "But I don't know . . ."

He awoke from the reading with a new buoyancy of spirits. "You were right, Gertrude. This was something I was meant to do. I can tell by the way I feel—light and happy and refreshed, the way I feel after a medical reading that has saved some child's life. If I listen to you, I'll never go wrong."

"If you listen to your Bible and your own heart, you'll never go wrong, Edgar."

A day or two later, in the middle of the morning, he abruptly lost his voice. There was no gradual dwindling away. He was talking to Gertrude and quite suddenly, when he tried to answer one of her remarks, he could only whisper.

"I've done something wrong," he whispered painfully. "This happens only when I've misused my gift. It must mean that I wasn't supposed to seek that information on world affairs. But I can't understand it. I felt so good and so right, afterward."

"Lie down," Gertrude said. "I'll conduct a treatment to help you get your voice back." She spoke with brusque matter-of-factness to hide the fact that she, too, was frightened.

As he lay down on the couch, Edgar had a moment's panic, wondering if the power to hypnotize himself had also been snatched away. He blanked his mind with an effort. Then darkness closed in.

Sitting by the head of the couch, Gertrude saw his eyes fly open as they often did. With practiced hand she reached down past his forehead, her fingers gently closing the lids to prevent the eyeballs from drying out, as she had learned to do on such occasions. Then she bent forward and made the suggestion that the circulation would concentrate upon the throat, removing the trouble.

Nothing happened. She repeated the suggestion without result, fighting to keep fear from her voice.

She said, then, "The body will speak in a normal voice and at a normal rate of speed, telling what is wrong and giving details for removing the causes."

There was no answer. Fighting her panic, she gave the suggestion to awaken. Edgar slept on. For half an hour she tried every suggestion she could think of, with no response whatever. She was fighting back her tears when suddenly Edgar awoke.

He sat up quickly and kissed her. "Don't look so worried, dear one," he said in his normal voice. "Everything is all right. It's wonderful, in fact. Losing my voice wasn't either a warning or a punishment this time. It was a means to make me put myself to sleep right away so I could receive a new experience. Gertrude, for the first time in my life I had a dream while I was in a hypnotic sleep. It was so real and vivid I know it has meaning for me."

His face shining with awe and wonder, he told her of this dream that would mark the beginning of a whole new era for him.

At the beginning of the dream, he said, he saw all the graveyards of the world. His attention gradually centered upon India, and he heard a voice saying, "Here you will know a man's religion by the manner in which his body has been disposed of."

The graveyards became the white crosses among the poppies of Flanders, and walking there were three boys from his Sunday School class. They showed him their own graves, told how each had been killed, and sent messages to living friends and relatives. While he talked there, a part of Edgar's mind was asking, "Is this spiritualism? Are all our dead really still alive on another plane of existence?"

He wondered if he could see his own dead son. Instantly he was viewing tiers of babies. In the third tier from the top was Milton, who recognized him and smiled. Edgar felt a sense of peace steal over him, erasing grief and fear.

Suddenly he was standing by the grave of an old flower lady from whom he had often bought bouquets for sick friends. She came and smiled at him. "Your kindness helped so many. You may not realize how much those flowers meant to the sick. But be patient with the children, for they are gaining much." Edgar was ashamed, remembering how often he lost his temper over the pranks and mischiefs of Hugh Lynn and little Edgar Evans.

Then she said, "Please do me a favor. Many months ago a man who owed me two dollars and fifty cents left the money at your studio for you to give me when you came to buy flowers. You were out and he left it with the girl who was your receptionist then. She put it in the bottom right-hand drawer of your desk and forgot all about it. Later she left your employ. The money is still there and I wish you would give it to my daughter. She needs it badly."

She left, and Edgar then talked church affairs with a man who had been, in life, an official of the Christian Church. In a few minutes he had awakened with his voice restored.

When he had finished telling his dream he sat in silence, shaken by the experience. He said at last, "I wish I understood its meaning. It bothers me."

Gertrude touched his cheek lightly. "Don't look so worried. It was only a dream, after all."

"I suppose so." He stood up and went to his desk. Under some papers in the lower right-hand drawer he found an envelope.

The name of the flower lady was written on the envelope and inside was two-fifty in cash. He stood for a long time, staring at it, saying nothing.

Chapter Twenty

EDGAR'S NEW READINGS on world affairs began to attract attention. Occasionally they were prophetic, as when they predicted the breaking up of the Western Front in Europe, the end and outcome of the war, the Russian Revolution. This latter reading said, "On the religious development of Russia will depend the hope of the world."

Much later, when the situation in Russia began to assume frightening proportions, people were disturbed by that statement. A reading was taken, asking if that earlier prophecy referred to Communism. The answer was blunt. "Communism is not a religion."

Sometimes the readings were pointed, sometimes intentionally obscure. In the matter of prophecy there was a constantly repeated warning that prophecies were rarely infallible, since a general pattern for the future was always subject to man's free will. In an important and widely circulated reading on world affairs, the power that moved through Edgar Cayce issued a clear statement of its principles.

The reading said, in part, "With man's advent into the world, personalities, individualities, began to find expression . . . With the present conditions . . . these have come to that place in the development of the human family where there must be one point upon which all may agree. . . ."

The reading went on, recognizing how impractical and impossible such a thought seemed. Then it delivered the simple, staggering answer, the solution to the turmoils between divergent peoples of the earth.

"The world, as a world, has lost its ideal. Man may

not have the same idea. Man—all men—may have the same ideal."

That ideal—the brotherhood of man—was reiterated in every reading, whether it dealt with global unrest or an ulcerated tooth. Having revealed its purpose, the force that moved through Edgar Cayce would not let that purpose be forgotten.

Through the years, Edgar had come to accept his uncanny medical knowledge as part of his strange life. Now, as he began to dip into this wholly new fountain of knowledge gushing out of his subconscious, he was once more overwhelmed by a sense of awe and wonder. He read the notes and shook his head dazedly. "How could I say all that? I don't even understand half of it."

No mounting score of triumphs could change Edgar Cayce or shake his simple humility. He was the same warm, friendly, human man, with his share of human frailties. He knew that he smoked a little too much, and stubbornly refused to cut down. He loved rich foods and overate and paid the human penalty. He saw no harm in the use of alcohol, though he hated the abuse of it. On a rare occasion, he sipped a drink as a gesture of hospitality, but he had no taste for it.

He was deeply religious, but no fanatic. His devotion to the Christian Church was based on the belief that each man should find the church that made him feel closer to God, and then be loyal to it.

Like any man, he could be stubborn, moody, wildly impulsive. The urges that had kept him broke in St. Louis in his youth never weakened. He would go out to buy one rosebush, recklessly order fifty, and wonder afterward what made him do it.

Yet for all his earthly humanness, there was a mysterious unseen force in Edgar Cayce that made itself felt wherever he was. Children loved him and followed him on the street. Strangers were forever opening conversations with, "I have a feeling I should know you. Haven't we met before?"

Without conscious effort, he made everyone he met feel a sense of warm, exclusive intimacy. A young woman who had been restored to health through the readings expressed her reaction. "He made me feel as if all his life he had been reserving one little niche that only I could fill." A man who had come as a total stranger to ask for a reading, cried, "I wasn't anybody he'd ever heard of, but I knew instantly that he *cared.*"

In the spring of 1919 he received a telegram from a distant cousin, a girl who had always sneered at stories of Edgar's power. Now she begged an immediate reading for her sister, who was pregnant, and very ill. Doctors had abandoned hope of keeping her alive long enough for her baby to be born.

The reading said the girl's life could not be saved. There were, however, medicines prescribed that would make her more comfortable and keep her alive long enough for a normal birth. After the first dose of medicine, the girl said positively, "This is Cousin Edgar's medicine. I know because I feel better already."

She lived without pain for forty days, gave birth to a healthy daughter and died peacefully within two hours afterward. Edgar never forgot the letter of contrition from the skeptical sister. But this was not the end of the story.

Some years later he happened to be in that town and stopped at the barber shop. A man was in the chair, being shaved, and his little daughter was playing around the shop. When Edgar sat down she scrambled into his lap and threw her arms around him.

The man in the chair sat up. "I'm sorry, mister. I don't know what got into her. She usually runs and hides if a stranger even smiles at her." To the girl he said, "Get down, honey. You mustn't bother the man. He isn't anyone you know."

The girl hugged Edgar tighter. "He is so. He was with me at the river."

Edgar and the father both stared blankly. The barber, who knew Edgar, performed introductions. To Edgar it was one of the most shattering experiences of his life. The man had been the husband of his dead cousin. The girl was the baby who would never have been born if Edgar's reading had not prolonged the mother's life.

He was with me at the river. The words and their vast implications haunted Edgar.

In December of 1918 he had received a letter that was to exert a profound influence on the rest of his life. This was merely a request for a physical reading and answers to a few questions on business matters. It came from the editor of a newspaper in Cleburne, Texas, who had heard of Edgar's powers.

Edgar had long made it a rule that he would give readings only for those in real need. The request had not established this. He wrote back and a correspondence developed between the two strangers.

In one of his letters, the editor stated that he was a firm believer in astrology. He asked for Edgar's exact time of birth so he could have his astrologer cast a horoscope for him. Edgar complied, mainly out of curiosity. In his private opinion, astrology, tea leaves, and the entrails of a black rooster all belonged in the same category of nonsense.

During the next two months he was dumfounded to receive twenty-one horoscopes from as many astrologers in different parts of the world. In true Texas style, the editor was no man for halfway measures.

Edgar skimmed through the horoscopes and was amazed to see how closely they agreed. Their general analysis of his character was a little too accurate for comfort. He stopped grinning and settled down to a careful study. Out of the confusion aroused in his mind, one startling fact stood out.

Without exception, every astrologer wrote that a brief conjunction of planets on March 19, 1919, between the hours of 8:30 and 11 P.M., would bring the right conditions for the greatest and most important reading of his life. Astrologers in England, South Africa, India, Singapore agreed in every detail on this point. Most of them urged him to use that period for a reading of tremendous importance to the world.

This was too impressive to be coincidence or fake. As always, he took his problem to Gertrude. Gertrude finally said, "Why not use that time to solve your own

most important problems: questions that have bothered
you from the beginning. If your gift is so important that
you were singled out from all mankind to receive it,
then the proper use and development of that gift to help
mankind must be just as important as some quirk of
politics that won't even be in the history books a hundred years from now."

They invited only two close friends, one of whom was
a stenographer who could record everything said. Then
they sat down to map the questions that would be
asked. It proved to be a monumental task, but at last
they had narrowed the reading down to a handful of
questions whose answers could have momentous significance to Edgar's future use of his power. Gertrude herself inserted one question born out of a secret worry
that had nagged her from the day she first heard of Edgar's gift.

As the hands of the clock moved on 8:30, Edgar lay
down and put himself to sleep. Gertrude opened the
reading with the formula that had been given them by a
special reading as the one to best harness Edgar's
power.

"You will have before you the body and the inquiring
mind of Edgar Cayce, and you will tell us how the psychic work is accomplished through this body, and will
answer any other questions that I will ask you respect-
ing this work."

By now they had both become accustomed to the curious use of the term "body" in medical and life and
world-affairs readings.

The response came quickly, "We have the body here,
Edgar Cayce—we have had it before. In this state the
conscious mind is under the subjugation of the subconscious, or soul mind. The information obtained and
given by this body is obtained through the power of
mind over mind, or power of mind over physical matter,
or obtained by the suggestion as given to the active part
of the subconscious mind. It obtains its information
from that which it has gathered, either from other subconscious minds—put in touch with the power of the

164

suggestion of the mind controlling the speaking faculties of this body—or from minds that have passed into the beyond, but which leave their impressions and are brought in touch by the power of the suggestion. What is known to one subconscious mind, or soul, is known to another, whether conscious of the fact or not. . . ."

The next question reflected a weight that had lain heavily on Edgar's mind and conscience from the very beginning of his reluctant readings. *Is this information always correct?*

"Correct," the force answered, "insofar as the suggestion is in the proper channel, or in accord with the action of subconscious or soul matter."

Gertrude's question, prompted by her deep, persistent worry: "Will this work hurt the body?"

"Only through the action or power of suggestion over the body. This body is controlled in its work through the psychical, or the mystic or spiritual. It is governed by the life that is led by the person who is guiding the subconscious when in this state, or by the line of thought that is given to create ideas of expression to the subconscious.

"As the ideas given the subconscious to obtain its information are good, the body becomes better; if bad, or wicked, it comes under the same control. Then the body should not be held responsible save through the body controlling the body at such times."

The question asked next had grown out of a mutual aversion to any idea not clearly defined in their basic fundamentalist religious attitude. They were prudes in spirit and deeply upset by the uncertainties aroused by the horoscopes.

"Do the planets have anything to do with the ruling of the destiny of man?"

"They do," came the unequivocal answer. It followed with a brief outline of astrology; then, "The inclination of man is ruled by the planets under which he is born. In this way, the destiny of man lies within the sphere of the scope of the planets. With the given position of the solar system at the time of the birth of the individual, it can be worked out—that is, the inclinations and actions, without the will power taken into consideration."

There followed an outline of planetary influences ruling Edgar's life, followed by an ominous warning: "Hence the inclination is controlled by the astrological survey at the time of birth, either—no middle ground for this body—very good or very bad, very religious or very wicked, very rich or always losing, very much in love or hate, very much given to good works or always doing wrong, governed entirely by the will of the body. Will is the educational factor of the body.

"The body should live close to the sea, and should always have done so. This body is strange to other bodies in all its actions, in the psychical life, in all its ideas as expressed in the spiritual life, and its stand on all matters pertaining to political, religious, or economic positions. This body will be either very rich or very poor."

The next question reflected a burden that had lain heavily on Edgar's consciousness ever since the time in Hopkinsville when he had reluctantly consented to accept a share of the proceeds from his readings. True, hardly a penny had ever resulted from that decision, but it weighed on him nonetheless.

"Can this power be used to be of assistance to humanity and also to obtain financial gain?"

"There are many channels through which information obtained from this body in this state would be of assistance to humanity. To obtain financial gain from these is to obtain that which is just and right to those dependent upon this body for the things of life—not those that would be destructive to the bodies themselves, physically or mentally, but that which is theirs by right should be obtained for such information."

The last question was a catch-all. They had fretted and worried over other questions until at last they threw in an all-inclusive finale. "Is there any other information this body should have now?"

"The body should keep in close touch with the spiritual side of life if he is to be successful mentally, physically, psychically, and financially. . . ."

Gertrude looked helplessly about. There were no more prepared questions, but the studio clock showed still nearly two hours remaining of the mystical moments in time that would never recur. She tried to think of other questions, more momentous, but her mind offered nothing. With a vague feeling of enormous opportunities overlooked, she gave the suggestion to awaken.

Edgar's first impression on reading the transcript was a sense of disappointment. Somehow, from the buildup, he had expected something earth-shaking, a tremendous revelation or a prediction of monstrous events. At first glance this simple collection of answers seemed innocuous.

He read it again and his eyes began to open. He cried to Gertrude, "Why, this is everything in a nutshell. It explains the dumb things I do sometimes, my crazy tempers, why I let myself be persuaded to use the power for wrong purposes so often. I'm a battleground between right and wrong, but it tells me how to guard my soul. It answers the questions that have worried me most. It tells me it is right to take fair pay for my readings and helps me chart my course ahead."

He avoided the subject of astrology. Long before, his strange dream had pointed to the inference that the dead did not vanish into nothingness or whirl away as angels, but lived on in another realm. This so shocked his fundamental beliefs that he had tucked the idea away in a closet of his mind. Now he put the subject of astrology in the same storehouse, not out of reach but out of sight, so that he would not have to stumble over it when he prowled the corridors of his mind in search of reassurance.

Chapter Twenty-one

THROUGHOUT World War I and long after the armistice, Edgar and Gertrude suffered an ordeal that tore at their hearts. By the hundreds, pleas poured in to discover the fate of soldiers listed as missing in action. Were they alive or dead? How and where had they died? Where were they buried?

From the start his power made it clear that such requests were not viewed with approval. A major reason was clearly implied. Edgar's limited time would be absorbed in a search for the dead while the living cried for his help. Said one reading, in part, "Such seeking through these channels is among those things that may be done, but when there is considered the amount and the type and the character of information that others seek, it is like sharpening a pencil with a razor."

A more spiritual objection was given in another such reading. "There are many things that may be done that are better left undone. For, while there may be given those things that might make for the easing of the conscious desire, yet . . . are these things needed?"

Edgar and Gertrude understood, but as parents who had known grief themselves, they suffered terribly. How could they explain to a sorrowing wife or mother that some agonies are better endured for the strengthening of her own soul?

Meanwhile his medical readings went on producing their endless wonders. One reading called for a medicine no one had ever heard of. A second reading named a druggist in Ohio who had one bottle left. A telegram to that druggist brought the answer that his last bottle had been sold long ago. Even Edgar was baffled and suggested a third reading.

"The medicine is there," was the response. It named a particular shelf in the drugstore. "One bottle was pushed to the back of the shelf and overlooked. It will be found there, behind a display of newer products."

This information was wired and an immediate response came back. "MEDICINE ON WAY BUT HOW DID YOU KNOW IT WAS THERE?"

In another reading, a lady was advised to take something called codiron. This was spelled out so there could be no possibility of misunderstanding. In a few days the patient reported that there was no such product as codiron. No doctor or druggist could locate it and no pharmaceutical catalog listed it.

Edgar took another reading which named a drug house in Chicago as the manufacturer. An inquiry brought a bottle and a bewildered letter. "How on earth did you learn of codiron? It is a brand-new product, just perfected. We selected the name only a few days ago, and have not even made an announcement of it."

But for every victory there were a score of bitter defeats. Doctors refused even to read a psychic diagnosis, druggists said the medicines could not be compounded, patients themselves began to feel better and abandoned treatments too soon. The need for a hospital for adequate supervision of treatments haunted him.

Then, with the war's end, David Kahn came home with a new urge to make Edgar's hospital dream a reality. His own young brother, Leon, had died while his frantic parents searched in vain for a doctor who would heed Edgar's reading. This needless toll must be halted at all costs.

"I've had a lot of time to think," he told Edgar, "and I've figured things out. We'll get the money you need where the money is pouring out of the earth—in the Texas oil fields. It will be easy to get backing when a reading tells us exactly where to find oil."

"Oh, no," Edgar cried. "I couldn't. You know what happened when I was persuaded to apply my gifts to the wheat market."

"You can," Dave said flatly, "and you will. Think a minute. That was gambling. For every gain, someone had to lose. Oil comes from the ground, not someone else's purse. Besides, this is to further God's own purpose through a better use of His gift to you. Don't take my word for it. Ask your own power."

When a reading agreed with Dave, Edgar's doubts changed to a wild enthusiasm. The squire was brought down to help Gertrude run the studio. Edgar and Dave went west—to Texas and oil.

Chapter Twenty-two

EDGAR'S REPUTATION was already known in Texas. When a demonstration reading correctly named the day and hour a well would come in, and even gauged the flow, there was a stampede to hitch oil wagons to his flaming star. The problem became one of eliminating would-be partners, which caused hard feelings among those left out.

A small company was formed with men who guaranteed that a major share of their profits would go into building and maintaining a hospital. A reading selected the exact spot. Leases were obtained and the drilling began in an aura of golden hope. Edgar walked in a daze and wrote letters to Gertrude that were almost incoherent with optimism. With David Kahn, the Jew of his old prophecy, the work was at last beyond the dark years.

While the drill bit thudded down, Edgar obliged the drought-ridden countryside with readings that located shallow wells in time to save crops and cattle dying of thirst. He located several oil wells that came in exactly on schedule. For some reason, their own well kept bringing up indications of oil, but no oil.

Men looked upon Edgar as a miracle man. A gaunt Texan came up to him on the street one day. "You're the gent who's supposed to know everything. I just want to know one thing, mister. When in hell is it goin' to rain?"

Edgar glanced at the cloudless, brassy sky. "Friday afternoon at four o'clock."

"It better," the Texan growled and went on.

Edgar stood rooted, his mouth open. Why had he

given that answer? It had come popping out of his mouth without thought or volition. What did he know about weather?

His worry changed to wonder at precisely 4 P.M. on Friday, when the heaviest downpour in the history of that section broke the drought.

The months slid into a year and went on accumulating. His letters to Gertrude became less buoyant, almost elusive in their lack of detail. Finally she sent fourteen-year-old Hugh Lynn to Texas to investigate. His report increased her fears. Other wells Edgar had located were producing. His own went on, showing only traces, and now there was mounting evidence of sabotage.

The readings, too, were becoming vague and evasive. A new theme appeared constantly. "Unless all connected with this project are in accord on the use of the money to be received, the oil that is where it was stated to be will not be reached."

As the strain shortened tempers, flare-ups revealed hints to Edgar and Dave that the partners had private ideas of how much of their profits should be wasted on the quixotic dream of a hospital. More sabotage brought suspicions and accusations within the group. A reading cleared that up. Disgruntled oilmen who had been refused partnership were trying to delay drilling until the leases expired. Then they could take over and finish the well.

The conspiracy succeeded. The partnership ended, broke and disillusioned. Dave had a few dollars left and a backlog of hope. Edgar found himself drained of both money and hope. He had flown too high, and the long trip down left him stunned and bruised in spirit.

Out of the blackness of despair came a letter from Mohr, the coal mine operator whose injury had ended the first dream of a hospital. Edgar's reading then had slowly restored him to health, but had warned that some day he might go blind as an aftermath of the accident, and had told exactly what to do if this happened. Mohr had eventually gone blind and, to follow Edgar's treatments, had fought off doctors intent on removing his eyes. His eyesight returned, and with it a memory of that old dream.

"The enclosed check will pay your expenses to my home here in Columbus, Ohio. My own fortune is gone, but I have contacts. I am positive we can raise the money here to build a hospital."

"Go ahead," Dave urged Edgar. "I'm heading west to see what I can do. I'll keep in touch with you."

In Columbus, Mohr was full of enthusiasm and plans for the hospital to be backed and located there. A reading said, with almost monotonous repetition, "Virginia Beach. The body should be beside the ocean, should always have been."

When Edgar awoke they handed him a telegram from Dave Kahn in Denver: COME AT ONCE. BONFILS, OWNER OF DENVER POST, GREATLY EXCITED. IF DEMONSTRATION SATISFIES HAS TREMENDOUS OFFER.

"I've got enough cash for the trip," Mohr said, "and I'll go along. This may be the big break."

Bonfils installed them in a hotel suite and brought a skeptical doctor with the address of an anonymous patient with an unspecified ailment. "Go ahead," he challenged Edgar. "Prove that you've got something genuine and the sky's the limit."

The reading humbled the doctor and convinced Bonfils. "You're my boy, Cayce. From now on you're the property of the *Denver Post*. I'm no piker, either. Your salary is a thousand dollars a day. Now here's the way we'll work it to build this deal up right. You wear a turban and take a real exotic oriental name. We'll give you a custom-built Rolls with a box for footmen in livery. You give your readings behind a big veil so the crowd can just barely see you. You never talk to anybody, especially other reporters. . . ."

Edgar got up drearily and left the room without bothering to answer.

They met in the hotel suite that was paid for until the following afternoon. Edgar had nothing, Mohr a few dollars. Dave could buy food for perhaps three more days. They were carefully working out a budget when there was a knock at the door and the squire burst in. "I got your telegram to meet you here in Denver. You must finally have hit the jackpot."

Edgar clutched his hair. "Meet me here? I only wired you that you could reach me here. That telegraph company."

They were still stunned by this additional responsibility when a new telegram was delivered. Forwarded by Gertrude, it was from the president of the Birmingham Woman's Club in Alabama. It stated that they had heard stories of Edgar's miraculous powers and offered a fat fee for a lecture and demonstration.

Edgar lifted a haggard face from his hands. "Tell 'em we'll accept if they'll wire transportation to Birmingham."

Dave jumped to his feet. "Now you're getting sense. I'm on my way further west but I'll see that you three get there."

All the way to Birmingham on the train, Edgar worked nervously over his first public speech. He was used to standing up before a church full of people and discoursing on the Bible. Now he was expected to talk about something few people believed and fewer still, including himself, could even try to explain. If the situation had not been so desperate, he would have fled from the very idea.

One terrified talk early in October turned into a triumphant stay of six months in Birmingham. Among the guests at the first demonstration was the skeptical superintendent of the Birmingham Hospital. At the conclusion of the reading, he rushed up and begged Edgar to give readings for many of his patients. Edgar complied happily, and the whole city began to resound with the wonder of his miraculous gift.

Edgar's fame spread, and one day he received a frantic telephone call from Nashville. A woman told him that in a moment of despair her sister had taken poison and was dying. Edgar had an immediate reading taken and telephoned the antidote back. The doctor in charge looked at the source of the prescription, blanched, and

174

went into hiding while he wrestled with his conscience and his stiff-necked scientific training. When he finally emerged to admit defeat, it was too late. The girl had died.

Edgar began to din his need for a hospital into receptive ears. A group of leading doctors got tired of hearing about the miracles of Edgar Cayce. They got together and issued a challenge. For a test they selected a hopelessly crippled, dying patient, an orphan who was in Vanderbilt Clinic, slowly going blind as his life faded. Edgar was not given either the name of the patient or his location until the moment of the reading; nothing was said of his condition.

He put himself to sleep and immediately gave a thorough and accurate diagnosis and a description of external symptoms. At this point one of the listening doctors laughed aloud. "This gent has more than I ever gave him credit for. He's the world's greatest mind reader. We doctors all know the patient and have diagnosed his case. This clever rascal is picking our minds and feeding our own knowledge back to us."

As the rest were nodding agreement, Edgar spoke up. It was one of the few cases recorded where he gave evidence of having heard remarks made by any but his conductor. He said sharply, "If we are reading your minds, tell us which mind holds this knowledge. Since you examined the patient this morning, there has been a new development. A severe rash has broken out between the first and second toes of the left foot. When you have verified this, and if you are interested, we will tell how this rash was caused, how it may be cleared up quickly and furnish details of an immediate brain operation that will relieve the pressure causing the present partial blindness which, unless relieved, will become total."

A committee of investigators, hastily dispatched to Vanderbilt to complete Edgar's exposure and downfall, returned looking slightly sick. The rash was unmistakably present. Treatments and operation were carried on as the reading detailed and the patient began to improve immediately.

All Birmingham was talking of Edgar's miracles. A

committee was organized to get the Edgar Cayce Hospital under way, and over $60,000 was pledged in a few days to see the work begun. A reading was taken to procure advice on the best procedure to make this a success.

The answer was growing familiar. "This work will succeed at Virginia Beach. The body should be beside the ocean, should always have been there."

The committee, its enthusiasm and its pledges, faded away.

Mohr went sadly home. Edgar and his father packed and began a fruitless wandering, giving readings and stirring interest, but getting no tangible promises of backing for the hospital.

Disillusioned, weary, and broke, Edgar headed back for Selma. It was 1923; he had been gone four bitter years, with nothing but graying hair to show for it.

Chapter Twenty-three

It SHOCKED EDGAR to see the eager-faced little Hugh Lynn of yesterday now a grave, mature young man of sixteen, in his third year of high school. Edgar Evans had been a toddler; he was a sturdy five-year-old now, with a nickname and a penchant for mischief. The nearest his baby tongue had come to his name was Ecken; now he was permanently Ecken Cayce.

Edgar studied him anxiously, with the same lurking fear he had known through Hugh Lynn's early years. "Is there, I mean, have you noticed anything peculiar about him?"

Gertrude laughed. "Ecken! Goodness, no. He's not at all like you were at his age. Any psychic power that wanted to get into him would have to catch him first, and that takes some doing. If he ever saw a vision, he'd take it apart to find out how it worked."

Edgar relaxed visibly. It was a vast relief to know that his sons were normal. He had been afraid that something of his own strangeness would be handed down to contort their lives.

He pulled Gertrude into his arms and held her tight, murmuring, "I'll never leave you again. What can't be done together won't be done at all. We were happiest right here in Selma, helping those we could and not trying to get too big. We'll do it again the same way, now."

A letter of announcement was prepared and mailed to a list of everyone who had ever had a reading or shown interest in his work. With some misgiving, a fee of $25 was tentatively set—after a reading approved it. This was far less than a medical specialist would charge for an examination and a diagnosis. It was high enough to discourage the curious, yet not exorbitant; and, of course, no one in need would ever be refused a reading for lack of money.

There was one serious problem. They had to have a stenographer to take down the readings, and that was no ordinary task. The ability to handle medical terminology was only a small part of the job. The curious language of the readings would drive an unimaginative stenographer mad. It had bothered a great many people, including Edgar and Gertrude. Some of the language would be clear and simple; some of it was what one critic called "rambling, redundant, ambiguous, and evasive verbal meanderings." Sometimes the language was Biblical. There was a constant, stilted use of "same" and "self" that harked back to archaic English. Sentences would begin, turn back on themselves, and bog down in a maze of syntax that would baffle anyone.

To later authorities, who made detailed studies, the reason seemed to be that the source of Edgar's knowledge was struggling to express itself in a language that was crude and limited. It was like Einstein struggling to explain relativity to a kindergarten class.

Through that summer of 1923 Edgar tried dozens of applicants in vain. Then one day in September a tall, attractive blonde walked in. She was Gladys Davis, the older sister of a girl in Edgar's Christian Endeavor group. She seemed vaguely puzzled at finding herself in the Cayce Studio.

"My sister says you're looking for a stenographer." She hesitated. "I—I had a different job in mind, but I kept getting the oddest feeling that I should come here first."

They tried her on a reading. Edgar and Gertrude took one look at the finished transcript and said, "You're hired."

Gladys eventually became one of the family and Edgar's second right hand. Like Edgar, she had been chosen for a peculiar service to mankind. It was not an easy service; it would never be.

A short time later a man walked in and changed the whole course of Edgar's life.

Arthur Lammers was a well-to-do printer from Dayton, Ohio. He was an earnest student of religious philosophy, occult science, and psychic phenomena, and what he had heard of Edgar Cayce fascinated him. He pinned Edgar down and the questions poured out of him.

What was the human soul? Where did it come from and where did it go? Why were we born and what became of us after death? Was man really a fragment of God, or only a thinking animal put on earth for a moment of time? Was man eternally damned or eternally blessed on the basis of his conduct during that moment?

The questions tumbled out. Edgar could only say, helplessly, "I don't know. I only know what it says in the Bible . . ."

"Don't know?" Lammers cried. "Man, you're a telephone plugged into a cosmic switchboard, and you haven't even bothered to call up and ask why you're here on earth?"

"I know this much," Edgar said. "I'm here to help others."

"Then help me," Lammers said. "I've spent years looking for the answers to life itself. I've dug into the mysterious religions of the East and all their modern offshoots and I still don't know. If half of what I've heard about your gift is true, Cayce, you can use your readings to solve all the esoteric mysteries."

"I don't know what they are," Edgar said, "but I'll try."

He was faintly shocked at the idea that mere man would have the temerity to peer around behind the obvious statements in the Bible in search of fuller answers. He had been raised to believe that he should understand as much of the Bible as possible and accept what he could not understand on faith.

But Lammers' excitement was contagious; Edgar's curiosity began to increase. A staggering thought struck him. Gertrude still insisted that only part of his power was being utilized, that a vast part of it lay dormant, waiting to be harnessed. Was this the purpose for which it waited? He had first used his gift to heal bodies. Dave Kahn's suggestion had carried him on into life readings that dealt with mental skills and talents. It seemed reasonable that this spiritual seeking would complete the trinity of body, mind, and soul.

Lammers had to rush on back to Dayton. He would foot all expenses and pay for the readings if Edgar would spend some time there, delving into spiritual mysteries.

"I'll be alone again," Gertrude said, "but I think you should go. What he suggests may be what we've been hunting for."

Edgar set off with his mind in a turmoil. He felt ashamed of himself, now that his eyes had been opened. He had been like a schoolboy who worries over the meaning of a word but never thinks to open a dictionary to find it. The problems that had fretted Edgar half his life might have been solved by readings in a matter of minutes. He reached into the closet of his mind and took out two of them—astrology and life after death.

His first readings in Dayton, with Lammers preparing the questions to fill in the gaps in his own knowledge, were so deeply shocking that Edgar's impulse was to run, and never pry again. Before he could accept any knowledge, he must first accept a belief that outraged everything in his nature, his training, and his fundamental upbringing—reincarnation.

He was horrified. "That crazy idea that after my body dies I might come back to earth as a worm or a mouse or a cow? The reading couldn't possibly have said that."

"No, no," Lammers said patiently. "That's not reincarnation; that's transmigration of souls, a kind of twist some Oriental peoples have put on the belief. Reincarnation is simply a belief that the soul is eternal. At intervals it allows itself to be born again—to put on a temporary physical body—in order to accomplish certain things. Does that seem so unreasonable?"

"But—but it's contrary to Christianity or the Bible."

"Is it?" Lammers challenged. "You're supposed to be

the expert on the Bible. Quote me one passage that denounces reincarnation, will you?"

Edgar floundered helplessly. "Well, anyhow, if it is Christian, why doesn't the Bible at least mention it somewhere?"

"Perhaps it does. How about the third chapter of John, where Jesus said, 'Except a man be born again, he cannot see the kingdom of God.'?"

"But that's only a symbol. It means a spiritual rebirth."

"It might, but the Bible doesn't say it's only a symbol. It states it as a clear fact. And remember where Jesus asked His disciples who men said He was, and they told Him some said John the Baptist, some Elias, or Elijah, some Jeremiah or some other prophet. Isn't that a reference to reincarnation? There were many Old Testament prophecies of John the Baptist. In Malachi it says the Lord will send Elijah the prophet before the coming of Christ. People asked Jesus if He were Elias and He told them Elias had come already and they knew him not. The Bible adds plainly, 'Then the disciples understood that He spake unto them of John the Baptist.' "

"Ah-ha," Edgar broke in triumphantly. "Then how about John, when the Levites asked him if he were Elias and he said he was not?"

Lammers smiled. "I'm a Bible student, too. I'll answer you with a verse from Ecclesiastes. 'There is no remembrance of former things; neither shall there be any remembrance of things that are to come with those that shall come after.' No man, not even John the Baptist, remembers past reincarnations. We'd just go on repeating the same mistakes from life to life if we did."

Edgar put his head into his hands and moaned, "I don't know. I just don't know."

"Take your time," Lammers said. "Think about it until you've made up your mind. We'll let the readings go until you feel on solid ground."

As he left, it seemed to Edgar his mind would never know peace and assurance. Out of his inner turmoil came the soothing memory of Gertrude's words, "You will never go wrong if you listen to your Bible and your heart."

He took his Bible to a nearby park. This was his one rock, his infallible guide to the path of righteousness. He read until dusk blurred the pages, and was even more shaken in spirit. He had heard it said that the Bible could be used to prove anything. This was wrong. Nowhere in all his reading could he find one verse to prove that reincarnation was not God's true pattern. If the idea were evil, then it was the only evil not plainly named and bluntly condemned within those pages. Against this were Lammers' parting words.

"Think of this, Edgar. Jesus said plainly that no man may enter the kingdom of heaven until he is as perfect as Christ was. Out of the multitudes of the earth, have any men, even the saints, been as wholly perfect as Jesus? What are we going to believe, then? That all men are damned, that heaven is empty, and that all our prayers and efforts to reach God have been in vain?

"But if we view each lifetime as one grade in a cosmic schoolroom of the soul, we find meaning and hope. The virtues we learn in this grade advance us, and go with us, to a higher grade until we reach that graduation day when we stand before the Master to receive his diploma of perfection."

The thought was shattering only because it was so simple and logical. Instead of demanding that vast portions of the Bible be accepted with blind faith, it invited man's intellect to keep pace with his soul.

Through a sleepless night, Edgar found himself flinching less and less at the idea that had so shocked him at first. If he could find, anywhere in it, a single tenet that outraged his fundamental faith, he could reject it. But he could find no point of conflict. And, most significant of all, the power that spoke through him had clearly presented reincarnation as truth. In all the years, a reading had never been wrong.

Lammers was waiting for further discussion the next morning—not to convince, but to clarify. It was Edgar's suggestion to take another reading. Out of this came further conviction, additional details, and a new word that was strange to him: *karma*.

"Karma," Lammers explained, "is a Sanskrit word generally applied to the basic law of the universe, God's law—probably the only real immutable law in creation. It's the law of cause and effect, action and reaction. As ye sow, so shall ye reap, is a common Bible statement of the law. He that killeth with the sword shall be killed with the sword. By that law, God is not the author of punishment. Man punishes himself. Whatever he does, good or evil, must sooner or later be done to him. As the Bible puts it, man must meet himself.

"And there's Biblical evidence for reincarnation. We all know that through history plenty of men killed other men with a sword and still died peacefully of old age. Either the Bible made a thundering misstatement, or that retribution so flatly promised in kind is not necessarily intended to fall within a single lifetime. The Japanese who commits hara-kiri today may be fulfilling the *karma* of a Roman gladiator of centuries past."

"Don't," Edgar begged. "Don't feed me any more right now."

Later readings, long discussions, and Edgar's own intuitive feeling of rightness completed his acceptance of this enormous new manifestation of his gift and its purpose. A reading suggested the formula to be used in summoning this vastly expanded form of life reading.

"You will have before you," the conductor should begin, and then he gives name and date and place of birth. "You will give the relation of this entity to the universe and the universal forces, giving the conditions which are as personalities, latent and exhibited, in the present life; also the former appearances on the earth plane, giving time, place, and name; and that in each life which built or retarded the entity's development."

With each life reading procured by this formula, Edgar's excitement mounted. Their value to the individual was incalculable. Readings on Hugh Lynn and Ecken were clear examples. One had been a research scientist in previous incarnations, but had let himself slip backward by becoming materialistic. The other was bluntly

183

warned, "You have a very bad temper. You came to grief because of it, both in Egypt and England, so you had better learn to control it now."

Under Lammers's guidance, Edgar used the readings to learn more of the pattern of the universe. He was told that between incarnations, the soul has access to all its accumulated knowledge and experience. It can evaluate its progress back to eventual oneness with God and choose for itself which body and which era will best help it work out its own *karma*. Once in that body, such knowledge is erased from the conscious mind and retained only in the subconscious, which acts as scorekeeper through that life period.

Lammer's life reading laid his intense interest in spiritual matters to a previous incarnation as a monk. Edgar's own deep religious feelings were traced to an ancient incarnation as a priest. His psychic power was born in a day when, wounded and dying, he had achieved the supreme effort of separating his mind from the agonies of his broken body. Later, he had abused his psychic gift to amass a fortune as a gambler. Out of that backward step came his present conflict between his yearning for material comforts and his unselfish desire to help others. Each temptation overcome, when he turned his back on a chance to misuse his gift for personal gain, he repaid a *karmic* debt and moved a step closer to perfection.

Lammers urged him to drop photography, settle in Dayton under his auspices, and devote his full time to readings, both life and physical. "This is your destiny, Edgar," he said.

"I feel you're right," Edgar said. "It took me a while to accept some of the ideas, but I finally have."

That night Edgar wrote Gertrude to sell or lease the studio and join him in Dayton. He hoped Gladys would come along. "I've tapped the rest of my gift, now. The road is clear at last."

Chapter Twenty-four

THEY SAT in a shabbily furnished apartment in Dayton—Edgar, Gertrude, and Gladys. Ecken was asleep. Hugh Lynn had remained behind with a friend in Selma to finish his school term. The three stared bleakly at a dime and three pennies on the table. It was all the money they had in the world.

Edgar broke the silence. "Ecken is taken care of. That leaves thirteen cents to feed the rest of us for the day. That's good for one bowl of soup and a stale bun down at the beanery. We've had hard times before, but this is a new low, even for the hard-luck Cayces—and those silly enough to stand by them."

"I made my own choice," Gladys said, "and I've never been sorry. I'm not hungry, anyhow, and my mirror says it's about time I dieted."

Edgar looked at these two who had chosen to follow him with unfaltering trust. Everything had been so wonderful when they first joined him in Dayton. Lammers saw to it that they had the best of everything and his enthusiasm brought many clients for both physical and life readings.

To his surprise, neither Gertrude nor Gladys had rebelled too much against the new doctrine. Gertrude had said simply, "I had a feeling it would be something like this that would make your gift whole and your life complete."

Overnight, everything collapsed. Lammers suddenly became entangled in lawsuits that tied up his business and his time. He was out of town most of the time, fighting desperately to save his own home from the flood of troubles. There was not a penny to spare for the Cayces or the project so close to his heart.

Rent was weeks overdue and eviction imminent. They had sent Hugh Lynn a couple of dollars for pocket money, to spare him embarrassment before his friends. They had insured a few more adequate meals for Ecken. Beyond that, there was thirteen cents.

"Let's spare the excuses," Edgar said, smiling. "The fairest way is to draw straws. Short straw gets the banquet."

He reached for a scrap of paper to tear up and froze at a knock on the door. They stared at one another, the same thought in every mind—the landlord with the eviction notice. Edgar sighed, shrugged, and went to the door.

A stranger smiled at him and pulled out a wallet. "You're Edgar Cayce, aren't you? My sister is in the hospital and a friend told me you could give a reading that would tell what was wrong with her and how to cure it. He said it would cost twenty-five dollars so I brought the cash. Could you do it right away?"

When the reading was over and their benefactor had gone, Edgar looked at them with a shamed face. "Oh, ye of little faith," he murmured, "thy name is Edgar Cayce."

The buzzer signaled the morning mail. Gertrude came back in a moment with an envelope. In it was a request for a reading and a check for $25.

Private readings, too, began to pick up. By the time Hugh Lynn joined them, the Cayces were not exactly prospering, but they were in far better financial shape than they had been before. Medical readings were still producing their miracles and their surprises.

In one, Edgar began, "Yes, we have the body. Nabisco."

He continued the reading without further reference to this odd interjection. Gladys was intrigued and wrote the applicant to know if there was any significance. A letter came back from the man's wife. "This is unbelievable. When my husband was a little boy, his nickname

186

was Nabisco. It hadn't been used for so many years he had almost forgotten it himself."

When finances improved a little, Edgar took a short trip to Hopkinsville to see his family. On the way back, on the first day of December, 1924, he had to change trains in Cincinnati.

He climbed down from the one train and saw the one he was to catch for Dayton standing ready across the yard. It seemed about ready to pull out, and Edgar was afraid of missing it and facing a long wait for the next one. He grabbed his bag and started to run across the intervening tracks.

He was dodging between two rows of standing freight cars when there was a wild screaming of a whistle and a switch engine bore down on him. After the first moment of paralyzing fright, Edgar put his head down and ran as he had never run before. He cleared the last box car and leaped off the track only inches ahead of the on-rushing locomotive.

Aboard his train, Edgar collapsed in the seat, shaking with reaction. His lungs burned from the effort and the chill air. Every breath hurt him all the way home and for months afterward. Gertrude wanted him to take an immediate reading, but a number of cases had come in and he took those ahead of his own. When he finally got around to himself, the damage had been done. A weakness had struck his lungs, to bother him the rest of his life and eventually contribute to his death.

Meanwhile a new group of enthusiasts was awakening to Edgar's deathless dream of a hospital. This, too, faded quickly when the reading repeated, almost wearily, "The work will succeed at Virginia Beach." This time it added the information that real estate at Virginia Beach would boom and gave a name, Van Patten, as one that would be associated with that boom.

Meanwhile Dave Kahn had been forced to drop his efforts for the moment and make a living. He had gone into the furniture manufacturing business near New York, but he was still an enthusiastic salesman for Edgar, his works and his dream. One of those he convinced was Morton Blumenthal who, with his brother, was a successful New York stockbroker.

Mort Blumenthal rushed to Dayton and obtained relief for an ear infection of long standing by a medical reading. A life reading reawakened an earlier interest in metaphysics and philosophy as virulent as Lammers'. When he heard about the reading that pinpointed Virginia Beach, he was doubly excited. Not only was this a site handy to New York, but it was overnight from the leading cities of the north and south, with enormous potentialities as a resort area.

"If that's where you're supposed to be," he told Edgar, "that's where you're going to be. I'm making money hand over fist right now and I can't think of a better way of spending some of it. Get packed and wait for word from me."

"You'd better not get involved," Edgar said mournfully. "Everybody who tries to help build my hospital winds up suddenly going broke."

Mort Blumenthal laughed and returned to New York. Almost immediately he sent expense money to join him and set up readings for a few friends there. A few days later he handed Edgar a check and a key.

"I've bought you a house at Virginia Beach. Better get down there and get settled fast, because things are going to be happening from here on." He was more enthusiastic than ever because that name, Van Patten, given in a reading in Dayton, had turned out to be a real estate man with a firm belief in the future of Virginia Beach property.

With mixed emotions, the little group had its first look at the promised land of the readings. Here Edgar would know his greatest triumphs, greatest service, and greatest heartbreaks. At the moment, standing where the trolley from Norfolk had dropped them, they would have traded their combined futures for train fare back to Selma, Alabama.

Their first sight of the ocean was frightening. Days of storm had turned it into a roaring monster that smashed at everything along its front. The village cowered against the ocean, miles long and a block wide, a collection of shacks and ugly Victorian monstrosities that, during summer tourist season, would bulge with vacationers. Now, in the fall, everything was dead and deserted. Their new home stood alone on a sand dune, blocks beyond the end of the town, on 35th Street. The only grocery store was downtown at 17th.

The house, drafty and bleak and unheated, stood alone in the area the readings had predicted would shortly skyrocket in value with the coming boom. That was fine for whoever owned any of the land. They owned nothing but sinking hearts and the realization that here they were completely at the mercy of one man's whim.

Edgar looked at the village of Virginia Beach and was sick with fright. If Morton Blumenthal's wardship went the way of all their other benefactors', there was not a single job opportunity or any way of making a living. He had never felt so completely trapped. . . .

Gertrude's cheerful courage was a tower of strength in the first days. She found jobs around the house, keeping everybody too busy for gloomy introspection until the storm broke, the sun came out, and the world took on color and hope.

They plunged back into readings with a new excitement, a breathless expectancy. They were explorers, pioneers in a whole new wonder world of the spirit, and every new glimpse thrilled them as it expanded the horizons of their minds.

A few requests, mainly for check readings, found them through the uncertain mail. Blumenthal beat a path between New York and Virginia Beach. With his reawakened interest in religious philosophy, he took over where Lammers had been forced to leave off. His wide reading enabled him to frame questions that developed their knowledge.

He was there every few days, and between times he was sending outlines for new explorations. His demand for readings was insatiable, and since he insisted on paying cash for every one, they found themselves suddenly prosperous. They bought a cheap car, and Edgar plunged into a lifelong struggle with the problem of keeping garden topsoil on the surface of Virginia sand.

A reading on Virginia Beach developed the full pattern of its future growth down to the last detail. They were told exactly the percentage of future population increase and land values, the location of future centers of activity and why they were there. "The sands of Virginia Beach are radioactive as well as rich in gold and other minerals important to life."

Every prediction has already come true or is clearly moving toward exact fulfillment. Over thirty years later, scientists prowled the beach with Geiger counters and other apparatus. Their report, released in 1955, confirmed the reading. "The sands of Virginia Beach, Virginia, have been found to be mildly radioactive and contain traces of gold and other elements."

During the long winter many of the more prominent names on their earlier lists began to crop up again as old customers found them. One was a scientist and inventor, who had used the readings to help him solve many laboratory problems. It may have been a suggestion from this man that turned Edgar's psychic knowledge toward the matter of world weather.

"There will be," said a reading, "for the next few years many changes of an exceptional nature in respect to heat and cold." The prediction spoke of the oceans growing deeper, of currents changing, of a notable shift in the whole weather pattern. It related extreme heat waves to sun spots, but added that a current theory of forecasting weather by measuring solar radiations would not prove successful.

Thirty years after that reading, scientists announced that all the oceans are showing a marked rise and three feet have melted off the polar ice cap since 1900.

A later reading on the earth's coming changes offered some specific and frightening prophecies. "The earth will be broken up in the western portion of America. The greater portion of Japan must go into the sea. The upper portion of Europe will be changed in the twinkling of an eye. Land will appear off the east coast of America. There will be upheavals in the Arctic and the

Antarctic that will cause eruption of volcanoes in the torrid areas; and there will be the shifting of the poles, then . . . so that land of a frigid or of a semitropical nature will become more tropical, and moss and fern will grow. And these periods will begin during 1958 and 1998, when there will be proclaimed those periods when His light will be seen again in the clouds."

This is one of the few Cayce prophecies that dealt with doom or destruction. Later readings projected those earth activities into the next century with even more shocking prophecies of change in the face of the earth.

Of course these things may not come to pass at all. Only time will tell. But it is a little disturbing to realize that in more than 15,000 readings by Edgar Cayce, checked, cross-checked and bitterly attacked by learned skeptics, the percentage of accuracy is incredible.

During this period, Edgar was experiencing more vivid, more frequent, and more significant dreams. But he was so busy with readings that told others how to find lost health, he neglected his own. One day he had a disturbing dream of getting into the tub for a warm bath, of turning on the hot water by mistake, and scalding to death in great agony. The dream continued while he viewed his own funeral preparations and burial.

"First and foremost," warned the reading, "the physical defects in the body need attention, or death may occur." This was prophetic; when his death finally did occur, the cause was pulmonary edema, commonly known as water on the lungs.

However, the reading continued on a more hopeful note. "Even though the physical body may be laid aside, the operation of the work as seen and carried on in this state will be going just the same. The impression, the lessons, the guiding forces, the direction and the help to many will continue, especially to those with whom the entity feels, in the physical, the close endearments, the close connections."

That prophecy has long since come true. Edgar Cayce's work is indeed going forward at Virginia Beach in the dedicated hands of those who knew and loved him best.

Meanwhile Edgar was too busy to worry about a remote future or a present ailment that was not actually incapacitating. The requests for readings were coming in mounting numbers, with life readings beginning to outstrip pleas for medical aid, although there were many of those. They poured out of him in endless variety, some stern, some whimsical, but all infinitely wise and helpful.

A woman was told flatly, "Don't call on heaven until you have set your own heart and mind aright. If it takes six months or a year to get yourself spiritually correct, don't take a dose of the medicine until you are spiritually correct. It will do you more harm than good."

To a man: "Live that you can tell *everyone* where to get off, but see to it that you get off at the same place."

In May, 1927, Edgar's dreams took a forward leap with the incorporation of the Association of National Investigators. Anyone who mistook this for an organization of private eyes was disabused by the motto: *That We May Make Manifest Our Love for God and Man.*

This was largely Morton Blumenthal's brain child: "To engage in general psychic research and to provide for the practical application of any knowledge obtainable through the medium of psychic phenomena." He envisioned a farflung network of students interested in the readings and in other psychic manifestations, all studying and contributing knowledge that could be put to practical use in everyday life.

Most important to Edgar, the vision included his hospital. Combined with it would be a group headquarters with a library on the occult, a vault to preserve copies of the readings, and a staff to study and correlate the data. It was unthinkable that all the vast knowledge coming through Cayce was meant to be used by one person and then forgotten. The right study of his thousands of readings would surely reveal knowledge of value to everyone.

Dave Kahn, who was an officer of the new organization, came down for frequent visits. These always made Edgar feel a little more comfortable and assured. Dave was practical. Blumenthal sometimes left Edgar with the confused impression of a man running in all directions at the same time. Now his vision had expanded to include a university to teach what the studies revealed.

In the spring, however, those energies came to at least a temporary focus with the start of construction on the hospital. The site was a great windswept dune overlooking Atlantic Avenue and the ocean in the exact area recommended by a reading.

Between reading sessions, Edgar prowled the scene, diving in to give a hand to workmen, touching the great piles of lumber to convince himself that it was really true. After the years of frustration, he could never quite shake off a feeling that some morning he would awaken and find it had all been a dream.

The money Blumenthal poured into the project was real enough; nothing was spared or slighted. The enormous frame structure had space for thirty hospital patients with extra rooms for those who wanted to stay for treatments or to join the study classes Blumenthal was forming. There was a fine kitchen, living quarters for staff and help, and a great porch around three sides. There were research offices and a fireproof vault in the basement to protect the readings and assembled data. Ten thousand dollars' worth of terraced lawn set off the structure.

Since the readings recommended all forms of treatment, the equipment included standard hospital machines, from X-ray cameras to sinusoidal cabinets. An area of the beach was reserved for sand packs, an idea presented by a reading. For certain ailments, the patient was bathed in sea water, then packed with hot sand to absorb the beneficial elements which had caused the readings to insist on Virginia Beach.

There was also a section of the physiotherapy department set aside for a purpose that brought noisy ridicule from skeptics. In 1925 readings had described two electrical appliances of unorthodox design and purpose.

One they called a radioactive appliance, the other a wet cell. Complete instructions were given for building these, and subsequent readings frequently called for the use of one or both in specific treatments.

The radioactive device consisted of two steel bars, separated by glass plates and surrounded by carbon strips packed in charcoal. Leads from the steel rods terminated in metal plates for attaching to various parts of the human body. When in use the steel box containing the device had to be immersed in ice water. The reading made an unsuccessful attempt to explain the function of the device, finally dismissing it with the statement that it brought the electrical vibrations of the body to normal resonance.

Engineers studied the device and snorted. It was, they said, nothing but a screwball kind of condenser dressed up with mysterious trimmings to impress the public. Nobody offered to argue the point at the hospital. All anyone knew was that, screwball or not, when it was called for and used, the patient invariably got well. The association is still hoping someone will make a more detailed study and explain why.

The same applied to the wet cell. This was basically nothing but a big battery, discharging a weak current through a solution of gold, iodine, and other elements. It made no sense whatever to anyone—except the hundreds of people it cured.

The hospital was dedicated with great ceremony on Armistice Day. The next day the first of a flood of patients arrived. From then on the sick poured in one door and the healed out the other in an endless stream. There was rarely an hour when a bed was vacant, and the waiting list mounted daily.

Dr. House had come to be chief of staff, and Aunt Carrie took over the duties of hospital matron. Edgar wandered the corridors in his spare time, pinching himself in disbelief.

Not that he had much spare time. Readings piled up until, in desperation, he added a Sunday session to his schedule. In addition, he was somehow finding time for Sunday School and Christian Endeavor work at the

Presbyterian church, and for Sunday lectures and Tuesday-evening classes. The fame of his work and of the hospital spread to distant countries.

The hospital laboratory was busy compounding new medicines whose formulas were given in readings. Day after day Dr. House saw weird and wholly unorthodox treatments perform their miracles. "We've got to keep a record of everything," he insisted. "Standard medical theory and practice says we're crazy—and by their standards, we are. But these things work. We've got to keep records and study them until we find out why they work. Underneath the mass of readings there are basic principles that can revolutionize the science of healing, if we can only isolate them."

The readings ranged into all fields. One named an unknown doctor and called him "the most talented heart specialist in the country today." Others would send patients to chiropractors, naturopaths, masseurs. A woman was told to go to her minister, another to a Christian Science reader, a third told bluntly to go home and examine her soul instead of worrying about her body.

Starting one reading, Edgar began, "Yes, we have the body." He broke off and said sharply, "Come back here and sit down." A letter from the patient's wife confirmed that at the time set for the reading, her husband decided suddenly to take a last check on the back door before settling down.

During a life reading he startled everyone by interjecting politely, "Would you mind stepping aside, please?"

Through an oversight, Gertrude discovered a new capacity in Edgar's power. As she was about to begin the opening suggestion she discovered that the patient, a man in Chicago, had not been notified to remain quietly at his address during the period of the reading. Rather than waste time, she tried a desperate gamble. "You will locate the body at this address *when he was last there.*"

"Yes," was the prompt answer. "We have the body here. Twenty minutes to six in the morning." It was then three-thirty in the afternoon at Virginia Beach, but the reading was finished without incident. Later the man reported that he had left for work at six in the morning. The reading was so highly successful in his case that he sent many friends to Edgar for help.

Edgar had worried about the price of readings. He finally had them reduced to $20 for a reading. Blumenthal had revised the application system. "You've never had trouble with the law, and we want to make sure you never do." Under the new form, the person applied only for a membership in the association. The protective paragraph read, "I further understand that I am privileged to apply for a psychic reading from Edgar Cayce, for myself or some dependent member of my family, and that in securing the reading I am taking part in an experiment conducted by the Association for the purpose of ascertaining the value of psychic information."

It made no difference to Edgar, as long as no one in need was denied help. Blumenthal was angry at him, anyhow. When the press of applications for physical readings got too heavy, Edgar had put them ahead of his benefactor's research readings into philosophy.

Morton Blumenthal was basking in grander dreams. His Atlantic University was taking shape on the ocean front across from the hospital. Dr. William Mosely Brown, head of the Psychology Department at Washington and Lee, was to head a staff of the finest educators available. Dr. Brown had come originally to expose Edgar as a fake, and had ended as a convert. He was now given a fat budget and told to make Atlantic the finest university in America.

While Mort Blumenthal poured out fabulous sums, Black Friday hit Wall Street. He laughed at Edgar's fears. "Depression or no depression, I'm still making money. Don't you worry about a thing but your readings and your hospital."

Edgar did worry. He watched the rising flood of expenditures creep out unchecked in all directions and it frightened him. Again and again the readings warned Blumenthal that he was falling into the paramount sin of acquiring knowledge without putting it to proper use. The warnings went unheeded.

Edgar began to feel like a man trapped on a runaway train that was plunging down a mountainside at full speed, heading for a dangerous curve.

Chapter Twenty-five

DR. HOUSE had been ill for some time, kept going only by treatments given in the readings, but they also warned him his body was too strained from overwork ever to recover. In October he died. He was replaced by Dr. Lyman Lydic, who had become an ardent follower of the readings in Dayton. Edgar's sister, Annie, came to replace Carrie.

Edgar awoke one morning amid the wreckage of all his dreams. The eternal fountain of wealth had at last dried up. The university collapsed, and because it had been made part of the association over Edgar's protests, it carried the hospital down with it. On February 28th, 1931, Edgar saw the last patients moved out before he handed the sheriff the keys.

He was stricken with despair, heartsick and lost. One abortive attempt to revive the hospital through the donations of friends and boosters died quickly. Everyone had vast enthusiasm, but in the depths of the depression, no one had any money. Edgar and Gertrude had even less than most.

In stunning succession they were dispossessed from the house Blumenthal had bought for them, and then from a second. They moved into a third, only to have it sold from under them. Edgar had loved that place. It was on a little fresh-water lake, only a short walk from the ocean and the heart of town, but teeming with fish. There he could fish and find a few hours of peace. More practically, he could supply food for the table when there was no money on hand. Perch was his favorite fish and the lake abounded in them.

But before this he had suffered one of the cruelest

blows of his life. At Dave Kahn's urging, he and Gertrude and Gladys went to New York to meet possible backers for a new hospital. Between meetings with prospects, they gave readings for local people who heard they were at the Victoria Hotel and swamped them with pleas.

During their stay, they met a Mrs. Bertha Gorman who was living at the Victoria with a woman companion. Mrs. Gorman was intensely interested in Edgar's work and begged for a reading. She was almost in tears when Gladys told her regretfully that every moment of reading time in New York was filled. She could only send her application in and await her turn.

On November 7th, 1931, the last hope of hospital funds fell through and they were sadly packing to leave for Virginia Beach right after a reading scheduled for afternoon. At the last moment, the reading appointment was canceled. Since they had a long wait for the next train, Gladys phoned Mrs. Gorman that she might have her reading after all. She went to their room at once without her companion, Anna McNamara.

When Edgar awoke, Gertrude and Gladys were crying, and his client was watching him grimly. He sat up, bewildered. "What's wrong? Did I say something to upset you, Mrs. Gorman?"

"The name," said his client, "is Conwell, Bertha Conwell." She flipped open her purse to reveal a badge. "New York Police Department. You're all under arrest for fortunetelling."

Dave Kahn got them out on bail. The trial was set for November 16th. A young attorney, Thomas Ryan, who knew of Edgar's work, volunteered his services for their defense. Edgar was too stunned by the catastrophe to think clearly of anything.

News was slack at the moment, and the papers seized upon the arrest as the excuse for a Roman holiday. As the traditional blonde secretary in a triumvirate, Gladys suffered the cruelest and broadest of innuendos. Every headline made sneering reference to Edgar Cayce, age fifty-four, and his blonde secretary of twenty-six. Tabloid photographers took pictures of the three every time they appeared on the street, then cut off Gertrude's photo so the result showed only Edgar and Gladys apparently enjoying an intimate stroll.

Edgar suffered torments over these attacks. It took the combined efforts of both women and all his friends to restrain him during his rages or to lift his spirits out of his deep despondency. He calmed down, then blew up again when one of the tabloids reported that he had demanded $70 for his reading and had been paid in marked money.

The trial itself was brief. Policewomen Conwell and McNamara denied signing the association application but failed to produce the one Gladys had filled out for the reading. There was no case at all. Judge Erwin listened to Edgar's simple story of his life and work, heard Dave Kahn's testimony, looked at a group of angry association members who had come to see justice done, and issued his ruling.

Whatever Edgar did, it could not be legally classified as fortunetelling.

The three went home, vindicated but bruised in spirit. Fortunately no one showed them Arthur Brisbane's widely syndicated afternoon column. In it he lashed out angrily.

"There is a magic in words," he wrote, "much in a name, despite Shakespeare's saying about the rose. Edgar Cayce, his wife, Gertrude, and their secretary, arrested for fortunetelling, were told, 'You must not pretend to tell fortunes, because you can't.' Things looked dark, but Mr. Edgar Cayce, who knows language, told the court, 'I am no fortuneteller; I'm a psychic diagnostician.' Instantly he, his wife Gertrude and their secretary were set free to diagnose psychically to their heart's content. When a lady asked, 'Is this the right time to make certain investments,' the psychic gave her a psychic answer. The law couldn't object to that."

Back home they took a reading that echoed the despairing cry in their hearts.

Why did this unfortunate setback happen? Why didn't the power give warning of the trap? The answer was noncommittal, almost indifferent. It remarked merely that a certain amount of scourging was necessary to the development of the soul.

The scourging continued with the notice that their rented house was sold and they must find another in the face of astronomically mounting seasonal rents. Hugh Lynn was home and very badly disturbed by the swift disintegration of not only all their hopes and dreams but even their domestic security.

He had begun acting as conductor for readings, and now he suggested one to ask advice on what to do. Edgar was too despondent to care one way or the other. He lay down and entered his psychic state.

To Hugh Lynn's first question as to how or where they could find a house within their means, the reading answered promptly: "Buy one."

Hugh Lynn's nerves were already ragged from the pressure of uncertainty. He demanded with heavy sarcasm, "What do we buy it with?"

"Faith," came the sharp answer. "There is a suitable house for sale directly across the lake. Go over and buy it."

After he awoke Edgar sat for some time, staring thoughtfully at the transcript of the reading. Finally he stood up and reached for his hat. Hugh Lynn asked, "Where are you going?"

Edgar looked at his elder son in mild surprise. "Why, I'm going over to buy the house."

The owner showed him around the property, which was known as the DeTreville house, and Edgar fell in love with it. It was a warm, pleasant, roomy place with dark green shingles and wide lawns. There were no houses anywhere near on either side. The lake, with a small dock, was at its back door. Directly across the street called Arctic Crescent was the beautiful new Star of the Sea Catholic Church.

"The right buyer can have this for five hundred dollars down," the owner said.

Edgar fingered in his pocket the few coins that represented their entire capital.

"I'm afraid even that amount is out of my reach at the moment."

"That's all right," the owner said. "We all get into a fix now and then. You look like the kind of man I'd like to see living here. Suppose you go ahead and take over and we'll set the final closing for one month from today."

They moved in and Edgar settled down to fish off the dock and to worry. The days moved into weeks, but not one dollar had been put aside for that payment. To the others he insisted stoutly, "Have faith, and everything will work out." Privately he mourned his own lack of faith.

The due date fell on a Saturday. When the mailman brought nothing, Edgar let despair take control and told Gertrude she might as well begin to pack. In midmorning the telephone rang and the voice of the owner said, "I'm sorry, but I'm going to be tied up on other business today. Let's postpone that closing of the sale until late Monday."

Edgar turned from the phone, his face radiant. "Never mind the packing. God is still with us."

Monday morning's mail brought a note and a check. The note merely begged them to accept an offering from one who had been restored to useful life by a reading. The check was for $500.

With his security insured for a while, gaiety burst from him, even in the midst of sober life readings. To a man interested in starting a shaky business, the reading warned, "You can't begin business on a shoestring—unless it's a shoestring business."

A prominent Hindu lecturer and philosopher asked how he could contribute to India's freedom and the brotherhood of man. The response was an exclamation. "This is a large order, my brother!"

To a man asking if his dead brother would reincarnate within his lifetime, a reading snapped, "That's his business, not yours."

A woman who had come to Virginia Beach to have a reading in person was startled to hear, "These disturbances may be eliminated, but if you do it haphazardly, you will get only haphazard results. You must be consistent—and what woman is consistent? You must be persistent—and most women are persistent."

Occasionally a reading could produce unintentionally comic results. In giving life readings, Edgar would start by counting backward from the current year to the year of the applicant's birth, frequently interjecting comments that revealed the scope of his clairvoyance. ". . . 1924, 1923, 1922 (quite an experience that year), 1921, 1920 (bad accident), 1919 (nice new house) . . ."

In the case of a woman who was present for her life reading, Edgar counted back to the stated birth year, then said after a silence, "We do not find the body here. Something is wrong."

The woman blushed and confessed she had not given her right age. When the correct birthdate, several years earlier, was given, the reading proceeded and was successful.

The Cayce files contain a number of odd comments or prophecies that are still waiting to be confirmed. Starting one life reading, Edgar carried his usual regression to birth, but at the year 1918 he interjected a curious comment with no bearing on either the reading or the person.

"Hmm," he commented. "Nineteen-eighteen. Many changes will come from and through the efforts of some of those born near Bury St., Edmonds, England, on the seventeeth of March in that year."

Perhaps some readers may run across facts that will throw a bit of light on that odd remark. Similarly, anyone with access to U. S. Army records during World War II might be able to confirm the basis of an experience Edgar had some years later.

At around 3:50 on the afternoon of April 29, 1943, Edgar was awakening from a reading when he suddenly said "Oh! Oh!" in a voice that indicated great distress. When he sat up, his eyes still held an expression of sick horror. "I just saw one whole company of our boys wiped out on the African front."

In another reading, Cayce described a tomb of records, housed in a small pyramid and containing priceless records of ancient Egypt and Atlantis, the lost continent. He described this as being located near one paw of the Sphinx.

Meanwhile, one indication of the change taking place in Edgar was the increase in number and significance of his dreams. All dreams, the readings said, have a meaning. "Consciousness is sought by man for his own diversion. In sleep the soul seeks the real diversion or the real activity of self."

The readings interpreted the deeper meaning of many of Edgar's dreams but they frequently urged him, and others, to look within the self for the meanings. One particularly memorable dream of his required no help with its interpretation.

He dreamed of climbing up to a chapel in heaven to pray. A custodian showed him a large room in the chapel that was jammed to the ceiling with packages, all beautifully wrapped as gifts and all addressed to people on earth. The custodian told him sadly, "These are gifts for which people have been praying, but they lost their faith just before the date of delivery."

Edgar understood that the gifts were talents and abilities latent within individuals, but so rarely called for.

A number of readings said that every person has the gift of psychic power to some degree, but the more that person is concerned with material gains, the deeper it lies buried. The gift reveals itself in hunches and intuitions, in ESP—extra-sensory perception—revealed by Dr. Rhine's famous work at Duke University, and in flashes of genuine clairvoyance. There are thousands of authenticated cases of clairvoyance in history, from Abraham Lincoln's prophetic dream of his own murder to Swedenborg's experience in telling a group of friends that a bad fire was menacing his own home hundreds of miles away at that moment.

Not everyone can be an Edgar Cayce, but there was one other psychic whose work paralleled Edgar's in almost every respect. Andrew Jackson Davis, the Poughkeepsie Seer, was born in 1826. Although he had only five months of schooling, Andrew had all the knowledge of the universe at his fingertips when in a hypnotic sleep. The only essential difference between him and

Edgar was that he had to be hypnotized by another person. During the eighty-four fruitful years of his life, Andrew Jackson Davis gave thousands of psychic diagnoses for the sick and readings on spiritual matters, as well as writing many books. At the age of sixty he went to college, got his degree in medicine, and became a practicing physician, using psychic diagnoses on all patients. . . .

Chapter Twenty-six

THE MEDICAL readings were going on unabated,
but now the life readings were becoming steadily more
popular. Many times people approached who were skeptical of the idea of reincarnation and ended stunned by
the mass of personal evidence. Reincarnation is not an
idea that can be proven empirically; it remains a subject
for individual acceptance or rejection.

One of the most striking examples came to Edgar
through a nursemaid who was concerned over the future
of the baby she was hired to care for. The socialite
mother paid little or no attention to the child. On her
own initiative, the nursemaid asked for a life reading.

"The entity has great potentialities, but strict curbs
are needed," was the warning. A previous incarnation
during Colonial times had this entity a minister who
amassed wealth and power by his talents. In his lust for
wealth, he went into the slave trade and persuaded
members of his congregation to forget their scruples and
share in his profitable slave enterprises. The *karmic* penalties could only be overcome by strong character.

The mother sneered at the reading and continued to
ignore the child. As it grew, the original signs of genius
faded until the boy became a complete imbecile, unable
to leave his oversized crib. This might have been mere
coincidence except for one thing. On Sundays, when the
nursemaid turned the radio to a sermon, the child would
listen intently while great tears rolled down his cheeks.

During this time Edgar's psychic powers were showing up at odd moments unrelated to the readings. One
morning he and Hugh Lynn were leaving the Virginia
Beach post office when they met a woman coming up

the steps. Although she was no one he had ever seen before, Edgar turned pale, told Hugh Lynn to wait, and raced after her. He spoke briefly, then came back. The woman stood staring at him with her mouth open.

"I just got the oddest feeling," Edgar explained to his son, "that she was liable to be killed in an automobile accident this afternoon. I apologized for upsetting her, but I had to beg her not to ride in a car today."

The next morning the woman came to their door, still trembling from shock. "I inquired all over until someone told me who you were. You disturbed me so terribly yesterday. I thought you were a madman, but I couldn't get what you said out of my mind. I'd promised to take a car trip with a woman friend, but at the last minute I backed out. My friend was in an accident and is in the hospital, badly hurt. Police say anyone riding in the seat beside her would have been instantly killed."

In this period, Edgar came to the outraged attention of a young minister in Chicago. The minister and his wife were both missionaries to China, and noted writers on religious subjects. Coming home one day, he was horrified to find his mother in raptures over a life reading. He skimmed through it and was aghast that she could even accept any doctrine so sacrilegious to an orthodox mind.

When he failed to undermine her faith, he snapped, "That man is nothing but a charlatan and a fraud. I'm going east, anyhow, and I'll make it a point to stop by and expose him."

He stalked into the waiting room of the house on Arctic Crescent, prepared for battle. Gladys met him with her disarming smile. "Do you mind waiting just a few moments? Mr. Cayce is on the telephone." Her eyes glistened with tears as she added, "It's a mother calling to thank him for saving her baby's life."

The minister waited, glowering, certain that he would face a man puffed with pride and ready to brag of his triumph. The call ended. As the minister stalked in, Edgar was sitting with his eyes closed, tears on his cheeks, murmuring brokenly, "Thank you; oh, thank you for another life."

In that moment of awakening, the rage died and the minister stayed on to become one of Edgar's greatest boosters. His mother met Edgar and later wrote a piece about him for a national magazine, introducing countless thousands to the person she called the Miracle Man of Virginia Beach.

The minister himself became such an outspoken advocate that he was called for an examination before a board of his church. He gave such a convincing defense of Edgar and the authenticity of his power that not only was he vindicated but members of the examining board later sought readings.

To the end of his life—and even afterward—experts were constantly arriving to expose Edgar's fakery. They could usually manage to look wise and "explain" most of the phenomena by one outlandish report or another. But there was one manifestation that came up repeatedly in readings and it left the investigators talking to themselves. This was the casual way a reading would toss off names and addresses of people thousands of miles away as if they were next-door neighbors.

A medical reading for a patient in Albany, New York, a city Edgar had never visited, gave detailed instructions for treatments to be administered by a doctor. Then it added, "Go downstairs to Pike, next door. He'll handle them for you." Subsequent investigation disclosed that there was a Dr. John R. Pike at 70 Chapel Street, Albany—right next door to the patient.

About this same time a young osteopath, Dr. Frank J. Dobbins, arrived from Maine to open an office on Staten Island. He was unknown and it would be some weeks before the new telephone directory would carry his name. Meanwhile he hung out his modest shingle and prepared to starve for a while.

Almost before his name was dry on the door, a woman and her daughter walked in. "You're Dr. Dobbins," the woman exclaimed. "You have no idea what a time I've had locating you. We just happened to see your name now as we were passing by."

"That's very nice," Dobbins said, mystified.

She held out some typed sheets. "This is a psychic

diagnosis on my daughter, given by that miracle man, Edgar Cayce, at Virginia Beach. He tells exactly what treatments she is to have and says you are the doctor to give them."

Dobbins had never heard of Cayce or psychic diagnoses. The very name smacked of superstition. He accepted the reading with considerable hesitation. His own name sprang out at him. To the question, "What doctor can treat my daughter?" the answer was "Find Dobbins. He can do the job."

The treatments detailed were a little unorthodox, but Dobbins reluctantly agreed to follow them. The girl was cured in record time. He sat around waiting for this Cayce character to contact him and demand a split of the fee. Nothing happened except more patients recommended to him by name.

Dobbins finally investigated and became an ardent Cayce fan. He soon moved his growing practice to Fifth Avenue, in Manhattan, and shocked his colleagues by announcing publicly that he used the readings himself for correctly diagnosing ninety-five per cent of his cases.

One day Solomon Kahn got a phone call from a woman who had been governess to his children when they were small. "You used to talk a great deal about a man named Cayce and his miracles," she said. "Is he still alive, and could he help someone in desperate trouble?"

Her brother-in-law had been an employee at Grand Central Post Office for many years. Suddenly he had turned sullen, then quarrelsome, finally violent. Doctors could give him no help and he was finally committed to the Rockland State Hospital as hopelessly insane.

Solomon calmed the woman, then phoned Edgar for an immediate reading. The first words were, "This man is in an institution where he does not belong. He fell on the ice as he left the post office three years ago, and injured his spine."

Simple treatments were detailed. The man made a swift and dramatic recovery and returned to his former job. Months later Edgar was lecturing in New York's

McAlpin Hotel when this man walked down the aisle. He introduced himself to Edgar. "I came to shake the hand of the man who gave me back my life," he told a cheering, deeply touched crowd.

These were the moments of Edgar's life that compensated for the heartaches and disappointments and jeers of the skeptical. He had need of such moments. Adversity would dog him throughout life.

In late November, 1935, Edgar, Gertrude, and Gladys went to Detroit as guests of a family who had become close personal friends after being helped by readings. While there they asked Edgar to give a physical reading for a little neighbor who was ill. Since her father was a hardheaded skeptic, they preferred to bypass him at the beginning. This was a direct violation of protective rules set up by the association, but Edgar was never one to quibble over rules when a child was ill.

The diagnosis and treatments were given to the father. He took one shocked look and galloped to the police. On November 30th the three were arrested for practicing medicine without a license.

It was a repetition of their trouble in New York. A reading told Edgar: "In the letter of the law you are guilty; in the spirit of the law, no." He was advised to ask for a postponement of the trail from January 21st to March or April as a more auspicious time and advised to accept all the legal help he could get—if offered voluntarily. Eugene O'Leary headed an impressive list of defense attorneys.

Again the trial was anticlimactic. Gertrude and Gladys were cleared of all charges. Edgar was found guilty but paroled in his own custody. He went home, hurt but not embittered.

Meanwhile he had known a great exultation when Hugh Lynn chose to cast his lot with the association, taking charge of the complex job of indexing and cross-indexing the readings to make the information generally available. In hundreds of individual readings on arthritis, for example, there would be certain treatments, medicines, and diets constantly recommended. Hugh Lynn plunged into the enormous task of compiling all such data into separate studies for each disease or ailment. The ultimate aim was for doctors and hospitals and laboratories to study and test everything to determine if they could utilize Edgar's readings in their war against specific diseases.

The life readings offered an even more complicated problem. The association is now making extracts and compiling all references on a particular subject. With over 15,000 readings on file, many running to a dozen or more typed pages, this is a monumental task. Preliminary studies have been published on such subjects as *karma* reincarnation, dream interpretation, development of psychic power, a history of Atlantis, the power of prayer, and many others. Books have also been published on child training, combining many life readings on the subject, and a compilation of readings on world affairs. However, the surface has been barely scratched and the task ahead would discourage a less dedicated group.

Meanwhile Edgar was being swept up by new sensations and new powers. He was on the threshold of the most important change of his life.

Chapter Twenty-seven

ON THE AFTERNOON of April 26, 1934, Edgar awoke from a reading and stared around with a look of wonder. "I saw something," he exclaimed. "For the first time in my life, I had impressions during a hypnotic sleep. Maybe it was only a dream, but I saw woods and water as clearly as if I were right there."

From that day on his awareness expanded swiftly until he became completely conscious in two separate states of existence. He was at last truly a dweller in two worlds, one physical and one spiritual. In time the barriers between these two worlds grew so thin that Edgar was often baffled over which was which.

After his first conscious impression during a reading, the sensations flooded in on Edgar with increasing sharpness. A few days later he reported that he felt himself standing aside, watching himself slip out of his body during the hypnotic sleep.

On April 24th, 1934, Hugh Lynn returned from a trip to Norfolk to find everyone in a panic. Edgar had been unconscious for a full hour without saying a word or responding to any suggestions. Three times he had been told to awaken, with no response.

"The only thing I know," Hugh Lynn said, "is meditation and prayer. That's been given often in the readings." He joined the others in an earnest, silent plea for help.

Edgar presently awoke and sat up, staring around blankly, rubbing himself between the shoulder blades. He had no remembrance of impressions, but after a couple of days of headaches and a generally dazed condition his spirits were elated. Prior to that reading he had, for almost a week, been moody and withdrawn, short of patience and temper. After recovery he was unusually sociable.

During a reading on May 1st he found himself riding on a most unusual train. The coaches were furnished in gold and white, with cloud-soft seats and an air of luxury. Passengers on the train were the evangelists Dwight Moody, Sam Jones, Stuart, and many others. All were on their way to a great meeting where John the Apostle was to preach and teach.

There was a great deal of casual conversation. Someone had warned Sam Jones, who chewed tobacco, not to get any on the beautiful cushions. Someone else remarked that he liked this train because he was permitted to smoke. Sam Jones said, "Well, things are quite a bit different from what I preached." Stuart agreed.

Moody suddenly spoke to Edgar. "You are not just like we are. You are not in the same place with us. You are on this train with us right now, but don't forget you have to go back, and don't you get too far away."

Edgar had a sudden feeling that if he did not get off before they entered the next tunnel, he would never return. He slipped away and re-entered his own body. Awakening, he recalled that all those he had seen had died some time before. He added regretfully, "I'm always about to hear John preach, but I never do. I wish I could hear him, just once."

Now he began to be quite conscious of his experiences during readings. He usually became conscious, first, of a spot of light. This acted as his guide, carrying him up through spheres of darkness peopled with horrible shapes and monstrous creatures, to a point where he emerged into bright light again.

He began to be aware of mounting up through layers of darkness to a hall of records where an aged custodian gave him the books he needed for life readings. On November 28th, he saw himself being carried up on a wheel "like the Rotarians have," spinning around a massive column until he reached the top. At times he was given a whole book to read; at other times the keeper blocked off certain portions, saying, "This you must not read. This information is forbidden."

His waking life began to be complicated by this intermingling of the physical and spiritual existence. Talking to his Sunday School class one morning on the Jews, he looked up to see a large group of white-robed figures stalking in to fill the whole back of the room. Afterward he saw spirit audiences for many of his talks and even for medical readings. It reached a point where he would come home from Sunday School and remark, "I had a full house today—only eleven real ones, but every seat filled."

Readings confirmed the reality of his vision. He was told that even in the higher sphere there was still a need for learning. His talks on the Jews had drawn spirit forms who were still gaining knowledge.

In 1938 he gained a priceless aide whose life story was not too different from that of others who associated themselves with Edgar and his work. In 1929, harassed by personal problems, Mae Gimbert had heard of Edgar and his work through a friend. She scoffed and forgot it completely.

A few years later, in a blind effort to run away from seemingly insurmountable problems, she fled to New York. Untrained for business, she made a bare living as a waitress when, one day in 1933, Dave Kahn and a friend happened to drop into her restaurant for lunch.

Dave kept watching her and finally spoke. "You don't seem to belong in this New York madhouse. What are you doing here?"

Something about his earnest interest made her blurt out her story. He got out a notebook and scribbled something. "You say your home is near Virginia Beach. Take this note to Edgar Cayce at this address in Virginia Beach. He will help you."

Mae was so impressed that she quit her job, went home, and hunted up Edgar. He studied her keenly, gave her literature on the association and its work, and dismissed her. With his prescience he recognized one who was not yet ready to admit a real need for the aid that was his to command.

Mae read the literature only as far as the price of $25 on a reading. She had $25 but no intention of wasting it on any such nonsense as a "reading" from a spiritualist. Once again she forgot the whole incident.

In 1938, her basic problems unsolved, she faced a complete breakdown and was told that nothing short of a major operation could save her life. Friends urged her to try Edgar Cayce for a medical reading. Her need was desperate; she went to him.

"I don't have any money," she said despairingly, "but people keep telling me you can help me."

She was amazed at the warmth of Edgar's welcome. A reading was given and her consequent recovery followed. When she began to regain her health she marched in with grim determination. "I want to pay my debt to you, but I'm still not making any money. Don't you have any work I can do around the association to pay back some of what I owe?"

Edgar smiled indulgently and created a job. Mae was a fine typist. He set her to copying readings for the files and for anyone who asked extra copies. She is still there, in full charge of records in the vault, carrying out Hugh Lynn's dream of coordination and research. No amount of money would tempt her to leave the work. In the prophetic words of the reading: "Many will be drawn to the work, but only those intended to carry it on will stay."

In time Mae discovered the source of an uncomfortable feeling she had had for some time. Edgar could read her mind. She began to realize that as he walked past her desk each morning he was garnering swift impressions of all her problems.

She discovered this by noticing that every time she was worried by some personal problem, Edgar would glance at her keenly in passing. Then, a few minutes later, he would stroll back and begin an apparently idle conversation. Within a few minutes that conversation would be swung around to exactly the subject of her worries. It was a little disconcerting.

Then there came a time when Edgar was bowed down under the weight of poor health and increasing worries. Many problems came up in connection with the association, and Mae felt that he should not have her personal burden added to his own. She practiced at home until she found that she could blank out her mind for a few moments. Thereafter, when Edgar went by each morning, she would carefully erase all problems from her mind. He would look at her in startled awareness, then come back later for talks. Each time she kept him closed off from her knowledge. It disturbed him, but the subject was never mentioned between them.

In 1936 Edgar finally yielded to pressure from his friends and asked a reading about the advisability of increasing the association membership fee to $50. There had been logic in the arguments. Edgar could not possibly cope with every request. Why not, then, confine his readings only to those willing to pay the higher price?

The answer was emphatic: "To increase prices in this or that manner is to become money-minded. No!" Edgar concealed a grin of satisfaction and went on giving away more of his help than he ever sold. He copied and kept near him a prayer suggested in a reading: "Here, Lord, am I. Use Thou me this day, this evening, as Thou seest I may serve others the better: that I may so love, Oh God, to the glory of Thy name, Thy son Jesus the Christ, and to the honor of mine own self in Thy name."

Chapter Twenty-eight

READINGS had warned Edgar against becoming impatient at the slow spread of his work. He must be content to watch it grow thought upon thought, line upon line, stone upon stone. He wanted to make the information available to those ready to receive it, but never force it upon those who were not.

Edgar tried to content himself, although patience had never been his major virtue. In his diary he wrote, "The good we do lives after we are gone, so only good must be eternal. Will be wonderful, then, to have the good we have tried to do as the clothing of our life hereafter."

Membership in the association was growing and new study groups were being formed across the country. The Bible was their basic study, with Edgar's readings as a guide to richer understanding. Hugh Lynn's monthly bulletin was a bond that held the groups together and fanned their interest.

In the early summer of 1932 Hugh Lynn realized one of his dreams by promoting the first congress of members, which has been held annually ever since. Crowds came great distances to spend a week at Virginia Beach, listening to guest authorities speak on a wide range of philosophical and psychical subjects, to attend classes and formulate new plans. Edgar's regular Tuesday-night Bible class was by far the most popular item on the schedule.

The enthusiastic crowd scattered out from that first annual congress to begin a private project of its own. A building fund was started to provide the association with permanent headquarters and Edgar with an office. There were no wealthy donors. More dimes and quarters trickled into the fund than dollar bills, but the trickle was steady. Some members tithed to help it grow. Others took extra jobs or staged special projects to raise money.

By 1940 there was enough to build a modest addition on the rear of the Cayce home. It housed a staff office, a library, and a fireproof vault to protect the readings. Edgar's headquarters with his couch and desk and ancient typewriter occupied a large, sunny room overlooking his beloved lake. Almost every square inch of wall space was covered with photos of family or friends, or with religious pictures. Over the doorway he hung portraits of Lincoln and Robert E. Lee.

The new addition gave Gertrude a little more freedom in her housework, but not much. Edgar was forever prowling back to talk to her or brew himself the strong coffee he enjoyed. If Edgar had little patience in his own nature, Gertrude had more than enough for two.

Sometimes Edgar would get up from an afternoon reading session and leave without a word. When he returned at dusk, morose and silent, Gertrude understood and left him alone. She knew that he had been out looking at the lost hospital, torturing himself with memories of the great good that had been done for a little while.

Over twenty years before, a reading had said that if the Versailles Conference succeeded, the world would experience a millennium. If it failed the world would see the same elements plunging humanity into a second and far more terrible war by 1940. In the fall of 1939 that great war broke in all its horror.

Hugh Lynn enlisted and crossed Europe with Patton's tanks. Ecken succeeded in getting released from his job and joined the army. Edgar was lonely, but both boys had married and left sons to clamber into Grampa's lap for his wonderful Bible stories.

Publication of a new story on Edgar and his work at this time swept the country, and overnight Edgar's mail mushroomed from a small bundle a day to bulging mailsacks, each letter a plea for help.

Again Edgar insisted on reading every incoming letter, and over the protests of Gertrude, Gladys, and Mae he lengthened each reading period and added to the number of readings. Starting at his customary 10:30 in the morning, he would often be still reading well into the lunch hour. Nothing they said or did could slow him down.

His impatience leaped on ahead of ritual. At times he would say, "Yes, we have the body," and race into a reading before Gertrude could give the opening suggestion. He frequently began answering questions before she could ask them. Nights he paced the floor, tormented by the thought of people needing his help. A new flood of requests for information on missing soldiers poured in to tear his heart. He was a father with two sons swept onto the battlefields and he knew the anxiety behind each request, but the power was adamant in refusing such knowledge.

He drove himself and tortured himself until, in the fall of 1944, he broke down completely. It was days before he could find the strength to take a reading on himself. Gertrude framed the questions out of her own anguish and fear.

"How can the body best free himself of worry and anxiety concerning the office routine?"

"Get out of the office," was the flat reply.

There was a nursing home in the hills near Roanoke, where readings had often sent patients. The man who operated it had the equipment and training to give the special treatments which the reading demanded. Edgar demurred, wanting to stay home and keep at his work.

"This would be preferable," the reading said of the nursing home, "to any place where there would be the anxieties from others outside. You may carry on the work—but commence soon." It added, "Go where you will have the treatments available."

"How long should I stay?" was the next question, and the answer was blunt. "Until you are well, or dead."

Edgar and Gertrude went to Roanoke, and for a little time Edgar seemed to be gaining. But he could not keep himself from worrying about those who needed his help and were forced to wait. Eventually he fretted himself into a stroke that left one side of his body paralyzed.

At Virginia Beach, Mae awoke one morning with the strong feeling that she should visit Edgar. When she got there, she saw the dark misery in his eyes. He was homesick for his house, his friends, his beautiful lake. She got on the telephone. The word spread and friends materialized with an ambulance, oxygen flasks, all the things he needed.

He arrived home just after Thanksgiving and was happier but no stronger, lying where he could look out over the lake and see the bass jumping at sunrise and sunset. On New Year's Day, 1945, Mae dropped in for her daily visit. Edgar managed his twisted, half-paralyzed smile and whispered, "It is all arranged. I am to be healed on Friday, the fifth of January."

On the evening of January 3rd, Mae stood by his bedside and saw him draw his last labored breath. Suddenly she understood what he meant. This miracle of healing would take place on Friday, as he had told her—but on the other side of the veil he had done so much to lift.

She raised her eyes then, looking out toward the sunset, and saw the final miracle.

In Virginia Beach and in Norfolk and up and down the coast, they still speak wonderingly of the phenomenon that accompanied that evening's radiant sunset. Suddenly, a shaft of bright red shot up like an obelisk from the disc of the setting sun. It reached almost to the zenith and lingered there, a monument in the sky, until long after sunset.

Three months later, on Easter Sunday morning, Gertrude Cayce slipped quietly away to join the man she loved. There was dark and terrible grief among those dear to Edgar and Gertrude. That grief extended across the world to members of the association and to the countless thousands alive and well because of his great work.

Out of that grief came a concerted determination:

Edgar Cayce must not have lived in vain. The great work of healing body and soul, of bringing enlightenment to those who sought it, solace to those who needed it, must continue.

There must be, however, no deification of Edgar, no teaching in his name. Over and over his readings had warned that there must be a submergence of personality, a teaching only of truth that would make all men better husbands, fathers, citizens. This must be done, holding only to the one law: Thou must love the Lord thy God with all thy heart and with all thy strength . . . and thy neighbor as thyself. No one ever exemplified that teaching more magnificently than did Edgar and Gertrude Cayce, who gave their lives to make man free of fear, of doubt, prejudice, hopelessness, and pain.

Hugh Lynn returned to his work with the association; Ecken continued in his chosen career, but was determined to probe scientifically the secrets of the wet cell and the radioactive machine. The study groups grew and expanded, association publications multiplied.

During the twenty-seven months in Europe, Hugh Lynn had met a young advertising man from Pittsburgh, Vaughan Shelton. Upon their return, Vaughan had a deep inner urge to join himself to the project. He is active in the publishing program and a member of the editorial board for the association. As many readings had stated, "Those who belong to the work will find their way to it."

In the spring of 1956 the work of the association bore its finest fruit. Through a totally unexpected gift, they were able to buy back Edgar's old hospital, reopen the vault, and begin the restoration of his dream. Out of nowhere came the miracles that no longer surprise anyone in the association.

A nationally known decorator asked if they would permit him to donate his talents to decorating and furnishing the new headquarters as a tribute to Edgar. They had many offers of materials. A building contractor long retired but restless wanted to take over the supervision of materials and construction on the huge remodeling job. Helpers continued to drift in—carpenters, masons, painters—a little bewildered by sudden inexplicable urges to lend a hand to the project. God's ways may be mysterious, but they can also be direct.

To those who knew Edgar best and loved him most, there is no regret that he didn't live to see his dream realized. They know well, from all he taught them through the years, that Edgar Cayce is still with them and inordinately happy at what they have done.

Today

Out of the wealth of material in the Cayce files grew the Edgar Cayce Foundation and its affiliated organizations, The Association for Research and Enlightenment, Inc., and The Edgar Cayce Publishing Co., all headquartered in the same building at Virginia Beach.

The Foundation is engaged in the gigantic task of indexing and cross-indexing the hundreds of subjects discussed in the readings. Because of their age, the papers are rapidly deteriorating, and they are now being microfilmed for safekeeping and ready reference. The subject matter almost blankets the field of human thought; from the value of peanuts to the building of the Great Pyramid; from how to get rid of pinworms to prophecy of the future.

The Association for Research and Enlightenment is an open-membership, non-profit organization chartered under the laws of the Commonwealth of Virginia to carry on psychic research. It is devoted to the study of the readings and conducts numerous experiments in psychic phenomena. It also cooperates with and encourages investigation by qualified persons in the fields of medicine, psychology and theology. The active membership of the A. R. E., as it is usually called, is made up of people of all religious faiths and many nationalities, including foreign countries. Strangely, they all seem to be able to reconcile their faiths with the metaphysical philosophy emerging from the Cayce readings. They come from all walks of life; there are doctors, lawyers, ministers, artists, businessmen, school teachers, students, working people, housewives.

The Association, governed by a board of trustees, conducts conferences at the Virginia Beach headquarters and regional conferences in New York, Dallas, Denver, Los Angeles and other large cities.

The Cayce Foundation and its affiliated organizations occupy a large, rambling, three-story frame building of shore architecture. Standing on the highest elevation at Virginia Beach, the building and grounds take up a full city block and face the Atlantic Ocean, a block away.

Hundreds of visitors come every year. Besides the library and offices, there are overnight guest rooms, a cafeteria, lobby, publications room and printing press. With the steadily growing membership and interest, a staff of 35 workers, mostly volunteers, handles volumes of inquiries, special requests, lecture announcements and literature. Visitors are shown about the plant and grounds with its broad, tiled veranda overlooking the ocean. Everyone wants to see the fireproof vault and the readings.

To the skeptic there is an appropriate answer: in the words of Abraham Lincoln, "No man has a good enough memory to be a successful liar."

67-8-2